When Britain Invaded Soviet Russia

WHEN BRITAIN INVADED SOVIET RUSSIA

The Consul Who Rebelled

by

Andrew Rothstein

The Journeyman Press

London & West Nyack

First published 1979 by the Journeyman Press
97 Ferme Park Road, Crouch End, London N8 9SA
and 17 Old Mill Road, West Nyack, NY 10994

ISBN 0 904526 33 X

Printed in Great Britain by
Interlink Longraph Limited, London

PREFACE

At the beginning of January, 1919, a few days before being demobilised from the British Army, I read in "The Times" newspaper the exchanges about intervention in Russia between Rear-Admiral J.W. Kemp, R.N., lately the British Senior Naval Commander in the White Sea, and Douglas Young, then still British Consul at Archangel. The Admiral's letters in essence reproduced the propaganda in favour of intervention against the Bolsheviks — denouncing them as enemies of civilisation — which at that time were daily advanced in the press, in Parliament and at public meetings. The Consul's replies were astonishingly bold in their outspoken condemnation of the policy of the British Government, in whose service he still retained an offical post.

At the end of February, 1919, the letters were reproduced in pamphlet form by the "People's Russian Information Bureau", set up in London by British Socialists. The pamphlet was entitled: "British Consul Replies to Anti-Bolshevik Slanders". By this time the Labour movement in this country was beginning to respond strongly to the "Hands Off Russia!" campaign against intervention, and sales of the pamphlet were a considerable success. Neither then nor for many years later, however, was it generally known who Douglas Young was by his origins, or what had happened to him.

Only in 1967, in consequence of an obituary notice in "The Times" and of my note giving the main facts (so far as I knew them) in the "Morning Star", was I asked on behalf of Young's widow to deal with his papers. This book is the result.

My deepest thanks are due to Mrs. Nina Young and to her friends, the late Leslie Webb and Mrs. Barbara Webb, for clearing up many questions arising from the study of Douglas Young's papers. I must also express my appreciation of the assistance invariably provided by the staff of the Public Record Office in London and of the British Library's Newspaper Division at Colindale. The Librarian at Young's old school, St Dunstan's College, London, was most helpful. Through the good offices of the USSR-Great Britain Society, the State Lenin Library in Moscow very kindly gave me access in London to a number of rare works by Soviet historians on the events at Archangel from 1917 to 1919, for which too I am most grateful. The Czechoslovak

Embassy in London kindly helped me to secure some precise references in the national archives of the CSSR for certain events in 1917-1918.

Information and brief extracts from Crown copyright documents in the Public Record Office appear by permission of the Controller of Her Majesty's Stationery Office.

London, March 1979

Andrew Rothstein

LIST OF ILLUSTRATIONS

(to be found between pages 68 and 69)

PROLOGUE

At mid-December, 1918, barely a month had passed since the end of the first world war. Great Empires had crashed in central and eastern Europe. Millions of men were still under arms: but in Britain hundreds of thousands of soldiers who had enlisted "for three years or the duration of the war" were turning their minds to demobilisation with increasing impatience, as reports in the newspapers and letters to their editors showed. Only in the borderlands and on the coasts of the former Russian Empire were British soldiers and sailors still killing and being killed, to the accompaniment of a violent anti-Bolshevik propaganda campaign in press and parliament. For months it had led to questions in the House of Commons and produced evasive Ministerial answers. But the continuing severe battles on the Western front, the voluntary suppression of nearly all news favourable to Soviet Russia and the heavy hand of the Defence of the Realm Act, all combined to prevent any real movement against intervention. The signing of the armistice with Germany on November 11 indeed made possible a change in this respect. Some meetings against intervention began. But the dissolution of Parliament on November 25, and the launching by Premier Lloyd George's Coalition Government of a "Khaki Election", designed to secure the return to power of "the man who won the war", greatly raised the volume and intensity of the anti-Bolshevik campaign — with its accompanying conclusion that western civilisation was facing a Bolshevik menace even more terrible than that of German militarism — "a danger as grave as was the invasion of Genghis Khan or Tamerlane", in the words of the Prime Minister's special mouthpiece, the "Daily Chronicle" (December 18, 1918).

In the very midst of this campaign — polling day was still a fortnight ahead — a remarkable article appeared on December 14, in the "Herald", the left-wing Labour weekly which in war-time had succeeded the pre-1914 "Daily Herald". It was headed: "Britain and Russia. By Douglas Young", and a preliminary note explained: "Mr. Young, as the British Consul, was in sole charge of British interests in Archangel from December, 1917, until the military occupation on August 2, 1918". The text of the article follows:

> "During my eleven years' service under the Foreign Office in parts ranging from the Equator to the Arctic Circle, I have seen how the

direction of foreign affairs is the close preserve of an exclusive class bureaucracy; and how matters vitally affecting international relations are decided by officials, often of minor rank, who, for the most part, have no first-hand knowledge of the countries on which they are experimenting, and who ignore, if they do not actually resent, any suggestions or advice from 'outsiders' who happen to possess such knowledge. The plea of 'State Secrecy' is used by this bureaucracy to conceal their blunders, which often involve the lives of thousands of people. Our diplomatic representation abroad is also the exclusive preserve of a caste, the members of which in most cases do not even speak the language of the country in which they reside, and who gather their knowledge within the four walls of their Chancelleries or in the Court or aristocratic circles which they exclusively frequent.

"In my three years' service as British Consul at Archangel during the war, I have seen the money of the British taxpayer squandered with the most cynical indifference by a similar bureaucracy established by other departments.

A Double Game

"This British Government played a dirty, double game with the Soviet Government in Russia. First they gave a solemn assurance, which was published over my name in the Archangel Press, that they had no annexationist intentions and that they would not interfere in the internal affairs of Russia. This was accepted by myself and by every man who read it, and who was not concerned with the niceties of diplomatic quibbling, as meaning that the British Government intended no military action against the Soviet Government. Then they stabbed that Government in the back by forcing a landing of Allied troops at Archangel under specious pretext.

"So far from the Soviet Government having violated the sanctity of the British Embassy at Petrograd, the Embassy no longer existed, as its personnel had ignominiously fled the country some months previously, and official representatives of the British Admiralty and War Office were abusing diplomatic privilege — to which, in fact, they had no claim — to organise, in conjunction with Russian counter-revolutionaries, under cover of the Embassy building, a plot to overthrow the Soviet *de facto* authorities in Archangel and elsewhere.

"The British Government, having completely failed to understand the cause and significance of the Russian Revolution and the ideals and aims of the Soviet Government, proceeded to suppress any news or any expression of opinion which did not coincide with their preconceived ideas, and was therefore calculated to expose that blunder; and, further, they proceeded to misrepresent and blacken every action of the Soviet Government, giving either deliberately untrue or evasive replies to the few independent members of all parties who have tried by questions in Parliament to extract the truth; though there is, of course, always the possibility that Ministers have not been allowed by their officials to know what was going on.

The Peril at Archangel

"The Archangel expedition, considered only as a military enterprise, and apart from questions of morality or political expediency, is already admitted even by its militarist sponsors to be an even greater fiasco than might have been anticipated. It is actually in danger of being thrown out into the White Sea, leaving the civil population of Archangel to the vengeance of the Bolsheviks. And this failure is due primarily to the fact that our naive authorities grossly underestimated not only the moral force but also the military power of the Soviet Government, apparently believing that in its stronghold at Moscow, 700 miles from Archangel, the walls of Bolshevism would fall to the ground at the approach from the White Sea of a few brasshats and a nondescript force of a few hundred men 'scraped together'.

"The danger of the moment is that this disastrous experiment, which has only brought ruin and death to the Russian classes in the interior whom it was naively intended to help, may be repeated in the Black Sea, nearly 1,000 miles from Moscow, with inevitably similar results.

British Prussianism

"I have seen in Archangel a British general acting toward the Russian population in their own country as despotically as any Tsar, and conducting himself as scandalously as any of those Russian generals of the old regime who were a common subject of superior criticism on the part of British residents in Russia. One can only conclude from this that the war against Prussian militarism has created a Whitehall militarism little better than the Potsdam variety, and a British bureaucracy perhaps less corrupt, but hardly less incompetent than that of St. Petersburg.

"I hate 'Bolshevism' — a product of reaction working upon national war-weariness and popular discontent. But I am convinced that the policy — or absence of policy — of the British Government as regards Russia is responsible for having strengthened 'Bolshevism' by forcing the Soviet Government to adopt cruel and inexcusable measures for its self-preservation, and incidentally for placing Russia still more under the heel of Germany and for slamming the door of Russia in our own faces against British political and commercial influence in that country. I believe that Bolshevik propaganda has had as much to do with the sudden collapse of Germany as our military operations. And I am afraid that at this moment, when the most urgent problems of domestic reconstruction are awaiting settlement at home, we shall fritter away our strength and resources in a vain attempt to restore order in the Russian Colossus; and that if we do this we shall sooner or later provoke an outbreak of Bolshevism in the United Kingdom, thus realising the aim of the extreme Russian Bolsheviks of spreading their ideas throughout Western Europe.

A New War?

"Russia cannot be invaded and conquered by a few thousand men. The distances are enormous: the difficulties are great: the Bolsheviks are strong and are growing stronger. It is not a question of 'restoring order' in Murman or the Crimea. It is a question at the least of penetrating to Moscow. That means war on a large scale — it may be years of war. It means the sacrifice of thousands of lives and millions of money, with heaven knows what purpose or result. There cannot be limited intervention. If it continues it must be on a large scale — with all the consequences that implies.

"There is another alternative. I believe that if a delegation, composed not of bureaucrats or militarists but of broad-minded representatives of all British political parties, were to meet a Soviet delegation in a neutral country, an understanding might be swiftly reached after a few hours' deliberation. And I believe that that understanding might be acceptable alike to our extreme Socialists and to British capitalists, whose sole interests in Russia seem to be to get their money back and to secure a field of making more.

"M. Litvinoff is reported to be in Stockholm offering to open negotiations. It is for British public opinion to see that the opportunity for retrieving a ghastly blunder and for removing a stain on our national honour is not missed."

The effect of this public denunciation of Government policy by an established civil servant, who had witnessed the very events he was describing, so far as Archangel was concerned, can be examined later. One thing should be said at once: that it was probably without precedent in the history of the British foreign service But at this stage it would be legitimate to ask, as many did without much success: who and what was the author of the article?

PART I

1

Douglas Young was born on July 11, 1882. In all that is known of his early life there is nothing to suggest that he would not turn out an ordinary middleclass professional man, with no thought of disloyalty to the accepted principles of British political life. His father, Charles Woodrow Young, was a responsible official at the East India Railway Company's headquarters in London, and retired as its Secretary, one of the most respectable positions in the City. Douglas was a delicate child and an affectionate son, who after leaving home wrote weekly letters to his mother for many years until her death. The atmosphere in the home was one of deep piety: his father sang in his Church choir, and the family attended Church of England services regularly. Music was an additional common tie: a friend spoke of their musical evenings with the mother at the piano, the father singing and the son (Douglas had no brothers) accompanying with his violin. In short, it was a typical London suburban family, with a typical London suburban address: "Sidney Villa, Breakspear Road, Greenwich", such as one may still see by the thousand in the middle class belt of Outer London.

Born into this station in life, Douglas had an appropriate education. After some years at a dame's school, he was sent at the age of 11 to a large public school for day-boys in south east London, St. Dunstan's College. It was — and is — like many other public schools, the successor to a fifteenth-century grammar school, in the parish of St. Dunstan-in-the-East, in the very heart of medieval London. Here he spent seven years, distinguishing himself in all the school sports: by 1900, when he left, he was captain of the cricket and lacrosse teams, captain of the Athletic Committee, a member of the first Rugby Fifteen, first in the 100 yards, 220 yards and hurdles races in the annual athletic sports. In December, 1896, he won first class honours in the University of London Matriculation Examination: in 1899 he received prizes for Latin and Greek: and he became editor of the school magazine. School photographs show him to the very end with a singularly open and ingenuous appearance, the very embodiment of Juvenal's "ingenui vultus puer, ingenuique pudoris". This all-round distinction was remarked generally. "The School is better because you have passed through it", wrote the (school-boy) editor of the magazine when Young went to Cambridge in 1900; "he is of the highest character for industry and uprightness, and his influence as prefect and athlete was always used for good", wrote the headmaster in a testimonial in 1904.

If I dwell with such detail on the characteristics of the boy, it is only because they bear a singular resemblance to what was said of Young in after-life — and indeed to what he did.

At Trinity College, Cambridge, he had a classical exhibition. After his first three years of study, Young, owing to some personal difficulties, had only third-class honours in the Classical Tripos: but one year later, in 1904, having passed some months in Paris and Hanover to familiarise himself better with French and German, he won first-class honours in both parts of the Modern Languages Special Examination — a result which predetermined his ultimate professional career. At the University he had again distinguished himself in athletics. Recommending Young as a school-master, his tutor, J.D. Duff, wrote of him that "his conduct was always excellent, his work careful and thorough" and that he was "a sensible, good-tempered man": Dr. H.F. Stewart (later a well-known University Professor of French), underlining Young's gift for languages, said that he was "well qualified morally, intellectually and socially for a responsible position as tutor or scholar".

During the next three years (1905-7), in fact, he travelled as a tutor with English boys (one of them the grandson of Charles Darwin) in several European countries.

At that time he spoke fluent French and German. A very few years later he learned Russian: later on he spoke Bulgarian, Spanish and Italian — and "at the age of 84 he was still reading Latin for pleasure", wrote his widow.[1]

Such qualifications were a great advantage when, in the summer of 1907, he entered a competitive examination for the British Consular Service, and passing it successfully was appointed a Vice-Consul in August that year. He reached his first post at Zanzibar on November 18, 1907.

He served in Zanzibar just over a year, until December 1908. On his work there, the only record is a letter of thanks six months later (July 24, 1909) from Sir Edward Grey, then Foreign Secretary, for his "zeal and industry displayed in preparing a full, thorough and excellent report on the trade, etc. of German East Africa."

On December 29, 1908, he had been appointed Vice-Consul at

1. I am greatly obliged to Mr. W. Thorburn, Librarian of St. Dunstan's College, Catford, for kindly showing me the volumes of the school magazine for the years 1893-1901: and to Mrs. Nina Young for letting me see the copies of her husband's school and University testimonials, as well as for a great many other personal details, used in this narrative.

Sevastopol. Here he met, through her English governess, Varvara Liukhnakevicha, the 20-year-old daughter of Major-General Alexander Liukhnakevich, a minor landowner in the Tula province and a relative of Hvostov, the well-known reactionary governor of Nizhni-Novgorod (later a Minister of the Tsar). They were married at Sevastopol Cathedral on November 13, 1910. Although, during a few months' holiday on the general's estate. Young was somewhat surprised, (as he wrote in after years) at the lack of any social amenities for the peasants — he was discouraged from offering any of them a newspaper, for example — it did not shake his belief in the essential civilisation of the Russian educated classes.

From Sevastopol Young was transferred, still as a Vice-Consul, to Bogota in November, 1910, acting also as clerk and archivist to the British Legation. From the end of April, 1911, until the beginning of March, 1912, however, he was Chargé d'Affaires there: and even after the new British Minister arrived, Young played the principal part in promoting the amicable settlement of a dispute between the Colombian Government and a British railway company in Central Colombia.[2]

On January 1, 1913, we find Young (after a brief period of leave in England) as Vice-Consul at San Francisco, but becoming Acting Consul-General later in the year. Directly the first world war broke out, Young wrote (August 26, 1914) to the Foreign Office offering 10% of his salary as a contribution to war funds: Grey wrote back the following month thanking him for this "generous offer".

Evidently in connection with the delicate balance of forces between Germany, Austria and the Entente Powers in the Balkans, Young's next move took place in the summer of 1915 to Rushchuk, in Bulgaria, a post which he had to combine with Consular duties at Bucharest, in Roumania. But this appointment did not last long, because Bulgaria entered the war on the side of the Central Powers in October, 1915. On November 17, the same year, Young arrived as "temporary Consul" at Archangel, a post which he was to hold for three years.

Thus his work in the Consular Service had been as typical of the young and earnest civil servant, winning the approval of his superiors by assiduous and conscientious performance of his duties, as his earlier years had been of the model public school-boy and serious undergraduate. There are no grounds for doubting his recollection, in after

2. Among Young's papers there is a letter of July 6, 1912, from the company's representative, thanking him warmly for this assistance. There is also a letter of April 13, 1912, in which the Minister is requested by Sir Edward Grey to convey to Young "my entire approval of the manner in which he has conducted the affairs of His Majesty's Legation during the time that he has been in charge of British interests in Colombia".

years, that what he saw while travelling overland from Bogota through Russia back to England — by the Trans-Siberian Railway — made him begin to think that a "political explosion" in Russia was inevitable. But such an idea was a familiar one among all thoughtful Englishmen in Russia, on the eve of the fist world war, without their drawing any conclusion other than that of a general sympathy with the cause of Russian Liberalism, preached in the Duma by the Constitutional Democrats (Cadets) — especially after the visit to Britain of a delegation of the State Duma in 1909 and the return visit of a British Parliamentary delegation in 1912.

2

Archangel province had been described by Lenin in 1899 as one of those where "the immeasurable stretches of land and natural resources are still being exploited to the most insignificant extent", but where the main local product — timber — was being exported chiefly to Great Britain. In fact, "this region of European Russia has served in this respect as an external market for Britain without being an internal market for Russia". Russian businessmen were then hoping that the new railway to Archangel would change matters in this respect.[3] But fifteen years later Harold Williams, a well-known British newspaper correspondent in Russia, still wrote that the "rich natural resources" of Archangel province, particularly its dense forests, were as yet "barely utilised", and vast areas were still "to a large extent waste lands", used chiefly as a region of political exile. Most of the land was unsuitable for agriculture, so long as the huge swamps were not cleared.[4] British shipping had assumed first place before the first world war, and exports of timber were still the largest single item in Archangel's foreign trade. Two-thirds went to Britain.[5]

Only in one respect did the province represent a substantial market for the Russian interior, owing to the poor quality of its land. Its average annual output of grain between 1909 and 1913 was under 40,000 tons, while its minimum consumption needs were roughly four

3. *The Development of Capitalism in Russia* (1899, in Russian), ch. 8, section V.

4. *Russia of the Russians* (London 1914) p. 396. See also *The Russian Year Book* (London 1913) p. 659.

5. Shumilov, *The October Revolution in Northern Russia* (in Russian, Petrozavodsk, 1973) p. 23. Of the 44 sawmills in the province, 26 were foreign-owned.

times as great: the balance had to be brought in from Siberia and the Volga. Hence, despite its enormous size — its area equalling that of Britain, France, Belgium and Holland put together — the province had a population of under half a million before the first world war, less for example than that of Birmingham (England). Nine-tenths of the people were peasants, their small villages dotted here and there along the rivers over this vast forest area. At least a third of them were village labourers with no working cattle or cow.[6] This accounted for the yearly exodus of large numbers to the industrial towns of the interior, either as seasonal workers or permanently, a feature already noted by Harold Williams.

The staple sources of income for the mass of the population were coastal fishing, timber-felling (primarily the occupation of the peasant labourers) and work in the sawmills, with peasant domestic handicrafts of various kinds — apart from what the migrants to Petrograd and other towns could send home. While average wages in European Russia were 240-250 roubles a year, in Archangel they varied from 130 to 200 roubles. The slightly higher wages earned by the 12,000 sawmill workers at Archangel (from 180 to 240 roubles a year) — working a 12 hour day — were outbalanced by much lower earnings on the docks, in river transport and on fishing boats.

The war had made some difference, indeed. While some 40,000 workers of all categories in the province had been called up by 1917, adversely affecting the sawmill industry,[7] the population of the city of Archangel was swelled by an influx of soldiers, sailors and transport workers from 43,000 to 72,000.[8] Large numbers of British and Russian ships, which had in 1915-16 brought in coal, metals, machinery and other supplies, were frozen in at the mouth of the Northern Dvina or in Archangel port, owing to weather miscalculations by the British War Supplies Department: Young, in an unpublished memoir, puts their number at 100. The number of railway employees in the province as a whole had grown from 35,000 in 1913 to 71,000 in 1917, owing to the successful completion in wartime of a railway line from Zvanka (not far from Petrograd) to the ice-free port of Murmansk in November 1916: on the other hand, the call-up of peasants meant that some 35% of their households had no working males left.[9]

---

6. Vetoshkin, *The Establishment of Soviet Power in North Russia* (in Russian, Moscow, 1957) pp. 6, 7, 15. Shumilov, *op. cit.*, mentions 6.6% of the land as held by the 70,000 peasant households, while the State and Church held over 90%, which yielded all the exported timber.

7. Axionov, *Establishment of Soviet Power in the Archangel Province* (in Russian, 1956), quoted by Mintz, *History of the Great October* (in Russian, vol. 3, 1973), p. 673.

8. Mymrin, *October in the North* (in Russian, Archangel, 1967), p.9.

9. Shumilov, *op. cit.*, p.35.

Thus the main specific features of the Archangel province, noted by Lenin nearly twenty years before, had not been materially altered by the war. What was entirely new was a problem with which Young had to cope later on: the great stores of industrial raw materials, semi-finished goods and munitions, bought abroad on war credits by the Tsarist Government and piled up on the Archangel quays (some of them far distant from the railhead) since 1915. This was partly due to the fact that transport into the interior in any case was totally inadequate in wartime conditions. These stores included 14,000 tons of copper, 5,000 tons of lead, over 2,000 tons of aluminium and as much of antimony, large quantities of munitions, as well as some 250,000 tons of coal.[10]

The town itself, as Young found it in 1915, is described in his unpublished memoir: "A human backwater, where people lived and did not rush: where pigs in spring and autumn wallowed in the muddy pools of all but the principal thoroughfares: where irreverent goats stripped and devoured the tasty placards from the revolving advertisement boards and outside the post-office and the police-station: while cows, wandering home on summer evenings from the common pasture, turned in untended at the gates of their respective owners. Nobody lived at Archangel except from accident of birth, banishment or business: and the banished included officials as well as political exiles of minor misdemeanour. During the short summer a few Norwegian steamers helped Russian sailing-ships of the coasting trade to bring in the winter's supply of codfish and herring, then fled from the icy grasp of the pitiless North. A British or German ship or two brought in coal enough for the needs of the port and the electric light station, or heavy machinery for the sawmills, or the manufactured goods sufficient to meet the demand of Archangel province" (apart from the timber-ships).

The recollections of a French officer, Pierre Pascal, who landed at Archangel in May 1916, may well supplement this picture: "A town of wood, very simply planned: two straight lines of low houses, along a street the end of which one can't see" (Baedeker's *Russia,* in 1914, said that the town "stretched nearly five miles" along the river bank). "Sidewalks of wood. Tramlines. Short streets at right angles, in which you can see the Dvina wharves at one end and the tundra at the other" (*Mon Journal de Russie,* 1975, p.30). A map of Archangel in the Public Record Office which was produced for the British forces that landed there in 1918 in fact shows some 24 such streets, starting from the riverside, crossing the main Troitsky Prospekt at right angles and

10. The figures for coal are given by Kedrov, *For a Soviet North* (in Russian, Moscow, 1927), p. 29. For the other stores Kennan, *The Decision to Intervene* (London, 1958), p. 17, quotes an otherwise unpublished U.S. memorandum of March, 1918.

ending very soon at the swampy open country. (W.O. 95, box 5422).

The invading forces themselves carried away no very different impressions. A British journalist briefly commented on the "strangely primitive streets" (Singleton-Gates, *Bolos and Barishynas,* 1920, p.11). Writing many years later, an American ex-soldier wrote in terms which recalled those used by Young: "Schools and Government offices of brick or stone, most of the others of logs...Substantial homes and public buildings, electric light and trolleycars—and board sidewalks, mud streets and open sewers that stank for blocks. Hulks of boats and masts and cordage and docks and warehouses on the front, with muddy streets behind" (Halliday, *The Ignorant Armies,* 1961, pp. 56, 57).

One must add that in fact at that time there was no main drainage in Archangel, and no general water-supply: people even long after the Revolution were still drawing water from pumps in the very centre of the town.

These were the conditions in which Young began his consular activities at 65 Troitsky Prospekt, a building forming part of the Anglican Church in the city, on the site of the ancient "English factory" founded centuries before. For the first two years of his work, Young had the usual duties of a British Consul (he was given that acting rank). A British seaman who had attacked a Russian Customs official on board ship: a coloured British subject accused of "stealing by finding" a purse, also on shipboard, and jailed without trial for several months without the Consulate being informed: Finnish carpenters, enrolled in England without preliminary consultation with the Russian authorities, taken off British ships as Russian subjects by the police: British officers upsetting small boats in the river by the wash of their motor vessels — such incidents, as well as the more familiar routine of issuing visas, charging fees for stamping documents, etc. would have been enough to fill up his time.

But there was also a good deal of friction with both Russian authorities and British officialdom over more serious questions. They followed from the peculiar position of Archangel as Russia's one maritime outlet in Europe — not only for normal trade but also for wartime communications — now that enemy countries, Germany and Turkey, respectively dominated the Baltic and commanded the Straits. What looked like an unexpected thaw, just after Young's arrival, led to a dispute over the disposal of three British icebreakers sent in from Canada. The Tsarist naval authorities ordered one away to Vladivostok against Young's protests, with the Russian Admiral on the spot asserting that the shipping would be able to enter and leave the port until the end of January. Moreover Young found the British senior naval officer, Captain (later Rear-Admiral) Kemp, who had had no experience whatever of maritime ice, supporting the

Consul's opponents. The result was that, when the severe frost returned, ships which might have got away were finally frozen in, "some loaded and ready to clear, others half-loaded or discharged", as Young wrote in his unpublished memoir. He could not blame the Russians alone: as late as the beginning of December, 1915, the British Admiralty despite his warnings sent off a ship for Archangel carrying an armoured car detachment, which had in consequence to lie at Murmansk for the whole winter until the Murmansk railway was completed, a year later.

Again, after abortive hints from the British Admiralty that it might if desired take over the port of Archangel and run it on British lines — a suggestion rejected out of hand, with sarcastic remarks about the British wishing to treat the Russians as the Germans were treating the Turks — a Ministry of Shipping Mission was sent out from London in the spring of 1916. Its duties were vague, and its composition — of persons unfamiliar with Russia, and knowing between them not a word of Russian — not only complicated Young's work, but earned it much ridicule among Russians and British alike. Its civil engineer "soon found that in the building of wooden quays and bridges he could teach nothing to Russians accustomed from childhood to wield an axe": and the obvious overstaffing of the Mission produced ironical Russian comments that there were clearly many Englishmen not liable to mobilisation, and that the English intended to "fight to the last drop of Russian blood". British sea captains held up in the port gave the Mission the music-hall nickname, popular at the time, of "Harry Tate's Navy".

Young's life in his understaffed Consulate was still further complicated, and his temper tried, by the successive arrival of mysterious personages with special missions, of which he was not informed until they found themselves in difficulties and had to appeal for his help. Such was a major, who spoke Russian perfectly but would not fit into any organisation, his sole duties being to check British munitions as they were despatched to the interior of Russia. Such was a Passport Control Officer in charge of a group of Russian-speaking British businessmen, given uniform for the purpose, who were "engaged in the search for 'pro-Germans' — except in high places". Such was the Ministry of Shipping Mission already mentioned. "Each did what he thought to be his business, and each left to the others what he could not or did not want to do himself. The result was not only much costly overlapping, but also a constant risk of unfulfilled gaps... With a unified or properly coordinated organisation, the same work might have been done, at a liberal estimate, with half the staff and at a third of the cost, and undoubtedly with far better results" (Young wrote in after years).

It can hardly be doubted that these experiences of officialdom, Russian and British, played some part in preparing Young for his experiences after the revolutions of March and November, 1917.

So however did his experience of the Russian upper classes as those historic events approached. He wrote of a conversation in his own house on the fashionable Troitsky Prospekt, a few weeks before the March Revolution. "Among the people present was a certain prince of a well-known family, attached as liaison officer to a British general at the head of the Supply Mission. The rest were mostly Russian ladies of the 'best' circles. Conversation inevitably turned to the 'something' which everybody vaguely felt was about to happen. There was not a word about the sacrifices which might be made for the alliance or for the war, or even for the Tsar; but there was much about the best method of securing their material interests against the impending catastrophe. One lady plumped for land, as an indestructible and therefore safe investment. Another pinned her faith on diamonds, as being of high value and easily transportable (those in the know reported that there was a regular 'run' on the jewellers' shops of Petrograd and Moscow). The prince, as the latest authority from the capital, recommended house-property, and stated with evident satisfaction that he had invested all his realisable wealth in real estate in Kiev. That was typical of the mentality of the time in the highest society."

Similarly, Young recalled a conversation in the drawing room of the wife of the Russian Admiral commanding the Archangel port — a patriotic and capable woman, "undoubtedly loyal in the real sense of the word to the Entente". They were talking of the Rasputin scandal "and the procession of degenerate or incompetent Ministers in Petrograd". He said (writing in 1923): "I can see this poor lady, now a refugee in Paris, rocking her head in her hands and hinting at the unspeakable 'something' which seemed to be inevitable."

When the "inevitable" came to pass in March next year, Young was among the few Englishmen whom it did not take by surprise.

Appendix to Chapter 2

Conditions at Archangel were considerably worsened during the occupation and the subsequent armed struggle, lasting for well over a year. The Allied troops had been withdrawn by the end of 1919, and the White regime they left behind was overthrown by the Red Army in February 1920. Most of the sawmills by then were not working: timber output in 1920 was only 6% of the 1913 figure. The Archangel-

Vologda Railway, along which some of the fiercest fighting had taken place, was heavily damaged. Many merchant ships had been removed abroad, and most of the river steamers, barges and tugs — used freely as gunboats and monitors in 1918-1919 — had been destroyed or required extensive repair. The total loss inflicted on the Archangel economy was estimated at 1,000 million gold roubles, i.e. £100 millions (*V.Kraiu Severnom,* Archangel, 1969, p. 107).

In the next twenty years much was done to restore and expand the town's economy. New sawmills were built and old modernised. Many factories manufacturing products new to the region were established by the middle thirties (cellulose, wood-hydrolysis and paper; rope and brick; soap, clothing and leatherworking; fish and meat canning). Six technical colleges, dozens of schools, a public library, a regional museum, a number of scientific research institutes, a theatre and many cooperative shops were opened. Piped water supply was installed. The town now extended over 20 miles up and down the Northern Dvina, and the population on the eve of Hitler's attack on the Soviet Union was 250,000.

Nearly 100,000 citizens of Archangel died in the battle between 1941 and 1945, either in the regular Soviet forces or as partisans in the occupied regions of the USSR. Their monument — a soldier, girl warrior and partisan, in front of a great sail symbolising the "city at the gates of the Arctic" — would be an outstanding example of public sculpture anywhere. But the region itself was not occupied by the enemy, and did not suffer the devastation of other areas. For this reason the city could not claim the resources to begin radical reconstruction and replanning until the 1960s. A visit by the present writer in 1977, however, provided an amazing picture of what had been done since then. Vast areas all round the city had been systematically reclaimed, one after another, from age-old swamps, and developed under very modern planning schemes. Handsome avenues and squares, many gleaming white blocks of flats, well-designed public buildings had appeared, and were being extended before the visitor's eyes. More than half the old wooden houses had gone. As late as 1936, housing space totalled the equivalent of some 22,000 apartments: in 1977 the total equalled over 92,000. Moreover, since 1970 district heating had been introduced in the new town areas, replacing the old Russian stoves with their vast outpouring of soot.

Along the riverside a broad granite embankment lined with grass verges now ran parallel to the former Troitsky, now Pavlin Vinogradov, Prospekt (named after the Civil War hero, vice-chairman of the city Soviet in 1918, who rallied the first volunteer forces that year to resist the invaders). There were now 16 technical colleges and three of higher education, while nearly three-quarters of the city's 240,000 workers had had a full (7 to 17) secondary education. The local newspaper, *Pravda Severa,* founded in July 1918, had a daily sale of 134,000: it was getting 25,000 letters a year from its readers, printing 6,000 — 7,000 of them. Two-thirds of the 450 deputies to the city Soviet were workers, just under half were women. Not less than one-third of all school-children in the Soviet Union, the local people claimed, used exercise-books made at the cellulose, paper and printing works of Archangel, and exported to nearly all the 15 Union (constituent) Republics.

On the day this writer left Archangel in July, 1977, the town paper published two significant items. One was that automatic dialling had opened for all telephone communication with Moscow and Leningrad, as well as with other cities like Vologda, Kotlas and Murmansk, hundreds of miles distant. The other was an invitation to boys and girls of 15 to enrol at "Middle Vocational Technical School No. 29" for a three-year course of full secondary education, together with training as car-repair mechanics, builders' carpenters, painters and plasterers, or crane-drivers, with full maintenance by the State, and good hostel accommodation if they came from outside Archangel.

A far cry from the Archangel which Admiral Kemp and General Poole had known.

3

The overthrow of Tsardom in Petrograd on March 12, 1917, made very little difference at first in Archangel. The economic and social conditions prevailing in the town and the province greatly favoured the "moderate" opposition parties — the Mensheviks and Socialist-Revolutionaries. The Bolsheviks, all told, numbered about 100. A mass demonstration on March 14 elected a committee to organise a Soviet, and during the next two days deputies were elected at all work-places. By March 18 there were 273 deputies, who chose an Executive Committee consisting of six workmen, three soldiers and three sailors. Politically its majority consisted of Mensheviks and Socialist-Revolutionaries, who were convinced as elsewhere that conditions now existed for class unity in prosecuting the war. Two of their actions brought this out in high relief. First, on March 16 the Soviet so far elected decided that the bourgeoisie in Archangel should be invited to form its own committees: and in fact the town council, elected under the almost mediaeval franchise system allowed by Tsardom, and dominated by factory-owners, merchants and large house-owners, proceeded to elect a "Provisional Committee" on the model of the Provisional Government in Petrograd, enlarging it by adding representatives of war industry committees and educational bodies. Secondly, the Archangel Soviet Executive, almost immediately after it was elected, issued an appeal to the workers "not to sharpen relations between the workers and the employers" by going on strike.[11] Thus Archangel, as elsewhere, had "dual power".

Young's (very fragmentary) diary for these first months reflects the conditions of the formal change-over at Archangel very clearly. "No police to be seen on the streets of Archangel" (March 14); "A large procession of workmen with the Russian (old) flag, singing the 'Marseillaise', came down town at 11 am" (March 15); after hearing a telegram from the Provisional Government, "the situation was quietly accepted" by a meeting of officials (the same day); "a parade of naval crews with flags 1.30 p.m. marching to the Cathedral" (March 16); "the police go over" (March 18); "soldier pickets with white armbands at street corners" (March 20); "delegates of Duma and Commissar arrive" (March 21); "Liberty Day. A great demonstration in Cathedral Square. General holiday. Kemp and Proctor make speeches" (March 23). Proctor was a British businessman engaged in the herring trade in peace time: in war time he had been organising the export of flax to Britain. From Young's notes we learn that both British speakers urged their audience to continue the war with the utmost energy. The Provisional Government in Petrograd had appointed the City Mayor its Commissar. On March 24 Young entered: "Called on Mayor and left cards for Duma delegation". The one event which might have caused him some disquiet at the time was entered on March 30: "Twentyfive Russian naval officers with General Forsel and Capt. Pedko are arrested by their men on their own authority, and will be sent to Petrograd tonight". But this action—evidently taken against officers who had rendered themselves particularly obnoxious to the sailors—was itself indicative of the prevailing moderation, compared with what happened to the most hated Tsarist officers elsewhere in those days.

In his unpublished memoir, Young gives another example. Commodore Kemp (as he now was) had been in Petrograd with Young's Vice-Consul when the March Revolution took place, and a few days later they travelled to Archangel:

> "The station at Petrograd was packed with soldiers deserting to their villages. In the hope of getting better accommodation the

---

11. These and other interesting details of the situation at Archangel immediately following the March Revolution are given by Mintz, *op. cit.*, vol. 3., pp. 786, 803, 821-2. The appeal not to strike is quoted by Mymrin, *op. cit.*, p. 15.

Senior Naval Officer, who was in uniform, passed himself off as an English 'Admiral'. Even so, they had great difficulty in boarding the train and securing two places in an ordinary compartment. The corridor was packed with soldiers, some of whom soon began to rattle at the door and then to poke in their heads, only to get them bitten off by the fiery 'Admiral' in the best pre-revolutionary manner of his kind. As the soldiers, who perhaps had not slept for days, began to feel worn out, their thoughts again turned to the new liberty and the empty places in the 'Admiral's' compartment; and in due course the previous hints that admission was desired were renewed in a more emphatic form. As the S.N.O. showed signs of boiling over and the soldiers looked like business, the Vice-Consul, scenting trouble, scrambled across to the international car and managed to secure the promise of one berth and the conductor's bunk. On his return with the good news, a strange sight met his eyes. The seats were occupied by two or three soldiers, while the 'Admiral' stood in the doorway and talked to them. It appeared that they had been slightly wounded in the disturbances in Petrograd. When the S.N.O. found that out, his better feelings came at once to the surface, and he had insisted on their coming into his compartment. They were obviously confused and ill at ease at being seated while the 'English Admiral' stood and ministered to their comfort. But the S.N.O. was as despotic in his goodness as in his wrath, and they had to do what they were told. In due course the train made the customary halt for a meal, and the British travellers adjourned to the station buffet. There the S.N.O., espying a great pile of bread-and-butter or similar eatables, straight away commanded the Vice-Consul to 'buy the lot'. This was done, and the food distributed to the astonished Russian soldiers, who would scarcely have associated that treatment even with the millenium...The incident showed at any rate what could be done by kindness. But kindness in this case came too late. The Russian soldiers were going home. They were on the whole quite good humoured about it, if rather forceful."

One other experience during this "Kerensky period" obviously made a deep impression on Young, though of a totally different kind. On May 1 he had gone on leave for Sevastopol, where his wife's family were living. On the way he stayed a short time in Moscow:

"There domestic servants — and comparatively few families in Russia employed more than a general servant — had to get up at 4.30 a.m. and stand in queue in the open street in order to get the morning supply of milk and bread, while their employers lay in bed. As soon as the morning meal was provided for, the maids

> had to drag off again to the market in order to get provisions for the dinner, and so on throughout the day. That sort of thing was bad enough in summer. In the mud and raw cold of spring and autumn, and in the biting frost of winter, it is a matter for wonder how the people endured it for so long. Prosperous and often thoughtless foreign representatives, living in the best hotels or enjoying special facilities, could form no conception of the economic position of the masses of all classes outside the wealthy few. Those few, on the other hand, had no scruple about accumulating hoards of provisions far beyond their needs, as was revealed when the revolutionary elements began to make domiciliary visits for the purpose of unearthing them".

And Young recalled frankly, after describing the growing economic disorganisation of Russia which had set in by the summer — and which he loyally attributed to the old régime, not to the Provisional Government — a striking conversation in July, 1917, with the Norwegian Consul-General in Archangel, who had spent many years in the country (his father had held the same post before him). "Why don't the Allies let these poor Russians go?" he asked. Young "produced the stock arguments from the English point of view about fighting the war to a finish, and so on". The Norwegian replied: "But they can't any more". Young asked him what the Allies could do under the circumstances. "Leave them to themselves" was the answer. "Say to them: 'Goodbye, dear people; we appreciate your efforts and your difficulties. But we have difficulties of our own, and we can't hang about any longer. We must leave you for the serious business on hand. But if we can be of service to you at any time, let us know' ". Young commented: "My patriotic feelings were ruffled, yet I felt in my heart that there was some truth in it".

Events, in which the Allies acted in precisely the opposite manner to that recommended by the sagacious neutral, were to deepen that suspicion, even though his patriotic feelings were not yet shaken.

The October Revolution in Petrograd also had only small repercussions in Archangel at first. After the rebellion of General Kornilov against the Provisional Government had been defeated, the Bolsheviks in the City Soviet on September 21, 1917, secured the adoption by 66 to 44 of a resolution condemning cooperation with the bourgeoisie.[12] But real power in the city and in other towns of Archangel province remained in the hands of the local town councils, which were controlled themselves by the bourgeoisie — and the latter enjoyed the effective support in the armed forces of monarchist and other professional officers. In the villages the Socialist-

---

12. Mymrin, *op. cit.*, p. 49.

Revolutionaries were in command. A "Revolutionary Committee" was set up by the City Council and the anti-Bolshevik groups in the City Soviet, and condemned the October Revolution, as did the newspapers under their influence. Only after days of fierce discussion did the Archangel Soviet, on November 17, adopt a resolution recognising Lenin's Government — but new elections, two days later, while producing a larger Bolshevik group in the Soviet, still left a majority of Mensheviks and Socialist-Revolutionaries. Elections to the All-Russian Constituent Assembly in December, again, while showing that the Bolsheviks had an absolute majority in the working class districts of Archangel, demonstrated once more that in the city as a whole, and in the province overall, the anti-Bolshevik parties had the overwhelming bulk of the non-worker votes.

Life at Archangel, consequently, was still proceeding on the old lines. Even as late as May 1918, when M.S. Kedrov, an old Bolshevik, arrived in the city as chief of a Government "Revising Mission", with a staff of 40 and backed by 33 Lettish riflemen, "it was difficult to believe that power had belonged to the Soviets for fully seven months". All the banks, Russian and foreign, were open: fashionable restaurants and beer gardens were flourishing: the institutions of Tsarist and Provisional Government days — City Council, War Industry Committees, Zemstvo Committees (representing primarily the small landed gentry, richer peasants and their cooperatives) — were in bourgeois hands and fully occupied: while the City Soviet was practically nonexistent, all its business being settled by its Menshevik and Socialist-Revolutionary majority jointly with the City Council. There, the Revising Mission established, nothing had changed since Kerensky days. Priests were being paid for providing religious instruction in the schools: church officials were being paid wages and fuel allowance; officers gathering in the city without leave were receiving rent allowance, and so forth. Interest on Tsarist loans was being paid out — all this in defiance of the Soviet laws.[13]

Not surprisingly, Young himself during these first months had no impression that any historic change had taken place. His (still very sketchy) diary noted (November 23) that the "Revolutionary Committee" had taken power in Archangel: we have seen already that this meant no particular change in the régime there. On the 24th, he noted that he had seen the President of the Archangel Soviet about the protection of British subjects and property. On the 28th, the French and American Consuls called "to discuss the situation". Two days later: "Kemp in with very alarmist views, wants me to send

13. Kedrov, *op. cit.*, pp. 10-11.

V. and other women home". On December 2: "3 women leave: the local paper prints statement about a general departure of all the English". On December 5: "Proctor returns (from Petrograd)": on the 6th: "Proctor with scares". About these references one must go to Young's unpublished and very pertinent memoir. Kemp was one of the "dangerous panic-mongers in the Allied Missions", he wrote. "He had served in China during the Boxer Rising, and his superficial knowledge of Russia led him apparently to think about the Russian masses in terms of Chinese Boxers. He had constant nightmares, not only of attacks upon Embassies and Consulates, but also of the outraging and murder of women and children". Proctor's fire-eating views will be found recorded in Foreign Office papers, further on. A close friend of his was another merchant, who because of his knowledge of Russian and Russian business methods "had become something of an oracle to the British naval missions on the subject of the real Russia which they did not know". After the March Revolution he became "a most pernicious panic-monger" and began "to see murder, and to breathe the same when out of hearing, against his former 'heroes in grey' when they declined to go on fighting on the Allies' terms". The October Revolution naturally increased his alarmism. "After jangling our nerves and distracting us from the urgent business of the moment by predicting our certain massacre, he needed little encouragement to follow the Allied Missions to more salubrious climes".

The ironical tones in which Young recalled these persons can be understood when we turn to what he wrote, just over a year after the events he described, in a letter to "The Times" (January 6, 1919) during his controversy with the same (now Rear-Admiral) Kemp. "As regards British residents at Archangel, I can state with authority that, so far from being at any time molested, they were accorded many privileges and exemptions to which they had no right; and I am certain that if they could speak their minds they would complain bitterly, not of the Bolshevists, but of the Allied diplomatic representatives, who themselves fled for safety to the cover of the Allied guns, leaving British men, women and children to take their chance of emerging from the on-coming waves of intervention" (Kemp himself left with the Allied Missions on December 17, 1917). Young continued: "We all lived for months under the dread of mob violence at German instigation, but I never at any time feared outrage by or with the sanction of the responsible Soviet authorities, so long as neutrality was observed: and I am glad of an opportunity of stating that I found the Soviet representatives at all times far more accessible and responsive to reasonable demands than the discourteous and overbearing officials who so often represented the

Imperial Russian Government".

This evidence was all the more impressive since Young had, after the first weeks already described, witnessed the gradual tightening-up of the political situation at Archangel, as the October Revolution began at last to take root there. On December 22, 1917, two local newspapers were closed for their persistent anti-Soviet agitation. In January a congress of sailors' delegates demanded the closing of all bourgeois newspapers: and it sent a detachment of armed sailors to the naval quay at Bakaritsa, near Archangel, where they disarmed and arrested 300 officers, setting guards over the stores of arms and munitions there. On January 31, 1918, after days of debate, the City Soviet elected a new Executive Committee, in which Bolsheviks came nearer to a majority of the 25 members: it closed down a Socialist-Revolutionary paper and dissolved the "Revolutionary Committee". The Land Decree which had been adopted by the Second All-Russian Congress of Soviets on November 8, 1917, was now applied in the Archangel province, and some 250,000 acres passed into the hands of the peasantry. They at last began to turn away in consequence from the Socialist-Revolutionaries. On February 17, 1918, the provincial congress of peasant delegates amalgamated with the provincial congresses of workers' and soldiers' deputies. The joint assembly declared its full support of the Soviet Government, elected an Executive Committee of 21 Bolsheviks and Left Socialist-Revolutionaries, 9 Right Socialist-Revolutionaries and 3 Mensheviks. It also decided to form units of the newly-created Red Army, and sent 10 wagon-loads of wheat and 100 barrels of fish to "hungry Petrograd". The threat of a German offensive, over the breakdown of the peace negotiations at Brest-Litovsk, brought a decision (February 21) to send 210,000 rifles from the Bakaritsa stores to Petrograd.[14]

4

None of Young's experiences, however, in any way affected punctilious execution of his duties as the senior — indeed the sole — official representative of the British Government at Archangel. The files of Foreign Office correspondence with him leave no doubt of this, or of his anti-Bolshevik attitude at this time.

---

14. Mymrin, *op. cit.*, pp. 69-89, *passim.*

On January 5, 1918, he reported that Somov, the Socialist-Revolutionary Governor of Archangel province who had been appointed by Kerensky and was still in office, had declared his readiness to hand over the war stores to the Allies in exchange for food-stuffs and other urgently needed prime necessities. Somov would not refer this question to the Soviet Government at Petrograd, but wanted a secret meeting with British, French and American military representatives at Archangel to discuss the matter.

Next day Young reported that, on Somov's initiative, a conference had opened at Archangel comprising (anti-Bolshevik) representatives of eight northern provinces — Archangel, Vologda, Olonetz, Vyatka, Perm, Novgorod, Yaroslav, Kostroma — ostensibly (Somov told him) to discuss economic problems "owing to the powerlessness of the Central Government". In reality, however, the aim was to "consider the question of autonomy" i.e. of revolt against the Soviet Government, in plain language. The weakness of the scheme, in Young's opinion, was the absence of any force to back it: but the organisers proposed to remedy this by organising a "militia of supplies", as a disguise for raising their own armed forces. Young underlined in his dispatch the great importance of the movement to Great Britain, as a means of countering German penetration, organising supplies of raw materials like timber, flax and coarse grains, and opening a market for British manufacture. "British support would not be directly invited, but would not be refused if offered", he added. Naturally, the Foreign Office (January 8) instructed him to keep in touch with the movement and report developments: "You should also take a suitable opportunity to let it be known that H.M. Government sympathise with the movement, and might if approached be prepared to give financial support".

However, on January 15 Young had to report that the delegates were afraid of provoking civil war, and consequently "the idea of separation found little support outside Archangel". While the leaders were "intelligent Socialists", mostly pro-Ally, they were "imbued with strong anti-capitalist principles" and thought that financial aid from, or concessions to, Great Britain would be "strongly suspect and should be avoided for the present". The psychological condition of the vast majority of the population was that they were "war-weary and hungry", ready for any connection which would "give them peace and satisfy their immediate needs at reasonable cost" — and he advised the British Government to take this very seriously into account. Going on to the general situation at Archangel, Young said that, while the "Revolutionary Committee" controlling Somov appeared to consist of "reasonable men", adopting the decrees of the Central Government only so far as expedient, the Bolshevik element

— chiefly soldiers and sailors — "must remain a potential danger so long as they control real force". The only policy which could hope to succeed, especially with the Socialist leaders and the masses, was to appeal to "local self-interest", which Young identified as food supply. He therefore advised (i) sending an official relief ship as soon as possible, with food supplies on terms of nine months' credit (ii) an offer to the "leaders of the movement" of a reasonable amount of food-stuffs and manufactured goods during the year, *even if Russia made a separate peace,* on condition that no raw materials from the territory should reach Germany.

However, no practical response came from London, which had other plans, as will be seen later. Young clearly had as many illusions about the attitude of his superiors as he had about the strength of the "reasonable men" trying to form an anti-Bolshevik movement in Archangel. By January 29 he had to inform the Foreign Office that the position of the Governor, and the "moderate Revolutionary Committee" was now seriously undermined. 3,000 Red Guards (i.e. armed workmen) had arrived from Petrograd, and the Sailors' Committee was demanding "full commissar control on the Petrograd model". On February 8 he reported the changes in the Archangel Soviet and the new Executive Committee described earlier, adding however that the "moderates headed by the Governor have largely succeeded in getting their own men elected" to the latter body, and could still "exercise a restraining influence". Increased Bolshevik control was to be feared as a result of financial aid to the local Soviet authorities by Petrograd; and the Governor "frankly admits to me that his only hope is to maintain some sort of equilibrium until the opening of navigation, when he would be glad to welcome British intervention" — a longing for which was on the increase, "not only in bourgeois circles but also among intelligent Socialists". However, on February 10 he told the Foreign Office that, by order of the Central Government, the post of Governor and Commander-in-Chief at Archangel had been abolished, and Somov retired: an event "imminent for some time". Archangel, he said, "must be now pronounced definitely Bolshevik, as that party now controls a majority of 2 or 3 on the Executive Committee of 25". Nevertheless he still hoped for "some sort of equilibrium" being maintained until the spring.[15] (In fact, it was not until June, 1918, that the Bolsheviks and their allies secured a stable majority on the Archangel Regional Soviet, as distinct from that of Archangel City.)

On February 22 the Foreign Office, "in view of the developments of the Russian situation" (which meant the German advance in

15. The four cables quoted here are in the Foreign Office files at the Public Record Office, Series F.O. 371, vol. 3305.

north-west Russia, because of the breaking-off of peace negotiations at Brest-Litovsk by Trotsky), took up with Young the proposal, originally mooted by Somov, for using food supplies as a means of getting the war stores at Archangel out of Soviet hands. These stores had been bought by the Tsarist Government on credit, to be paid for *after the war*: but the British Government adopted the very dubious position that, as they had not been paid for *already*, they remained Allied property. The ostensible reason advanced was that there existed otherwise a danger of the stores falling into German hands. But in fact the German armies were hundreds of miles away across difficult country, and documents subsequently published (as will be seen later) show that in reality it was Soviet possession of the stores that worried the Allies — which the Soviet authorities were sure of, from the start.

The Foreign Office cable (in the volume just quoted) said that the British Government was prepared forthwith to send three ships laden with prime necessities (coffee, salt, Iceland herrings, rice and cement) to Murmansk, to be kept there until four ships now at Archangel arrived with a load of war stores, and thereafter a shuttle service would be maintained so long as any of the commodities remained at Murmansk. But they wanted "if possible" not to bring the Central Government at Petrograd into the negotiations, and asked Young to persuade the local authorities at Archangel to "negotiate independently". In his reply, on February 25, Young pointed out the practical difficulties in the way of this scheme before navigation opened in the spring, and asked — significantly, it must be said — whether "in the event of the desire here being expressed to retain the metals, etc. for use in Russian industries, which I anticipate, do you wish the argument of *de jure* ownership to be pressed?" Just as significantly, no reply came to this enquiry.

From this moment the atmosphere became steadily more oppressive.

The state of mind among Young's superiors at this time can be judged from their comments on his cable of February 27 about the 210,000 rifles despatched to Petrograd, mentioned previously. The country had been called upon to prepare for total resistance to any further German advance, and the new Red Army had already won a minor success at Pskov on February 23 (since adopted as Red Army Day). But one official commented: "They will presumably end in enemy hands, like everything else we have sent to Russia", Another wrote: "At least they are intended for use against the enemy". His superior, in turn, remarked: "I do not know what grounds there are for this sanguine view". Both "H" (Lord Hardinge of Penshurst, the Under-Secretary of State) and "A.J.B." (Foreign Secretary Balfour) appended their initials without comment, i.e. without dissent.[16]

On March 4, 1918, Young sent a formal note to the Soviet authorities at Archangel informing them that the British Government regarded the war stores at Archangel as "exclusively the property of the Allies, not of Russia", and did not recognise the legality of the Soviet Government's decree annulling foreign loans (quoted by Kedrov, *op.cit.*, pp. 7-8). However, in a cable to the Foreign Office on March 12 Young insisted that (i) the stores could not be moved away by sea, in any case, for another six weeks. (ii) the Soviet authorities' programme was to deal with agricultural machinery and civilian supplies, "leaving genuine war stores until the last" (iii) any attempt to put pressure on the local Soviet at present would prejudice rather than promote British interests.

But the British authorities now began to exercise just that pressure which Young deprecated. A long despatch from the Foreign Office, dated March 18, informed him that, long before navigation reopened, there was the danger of the most valuable stores "probably falling into German hands" (the despatch did not inform him how this was known). He was directed to let it be publicly known in Archangel that (i) the British and American Governments had already collected and shipped for Archangel a considerable quantity of food, clothing and other necessaries (ii) as they had heard, valuable military stores "belonging to the Allies" were being removed from Archangel, "and will in all probabilities fall into the hands of our enemies" (iii) if the inhabitants of Archangel wished for Allied help now or in the future, "they must not permit action which is so harmful to us and so helpful to our enemies". Young was to inform the Foreign Office of the result of this proclamation. Meanwhile, he was told, two food ships would go to Murmansk and would be sent on to Archangel, "with the armed ice-breaker *Alexander*, supported if circumstances permit by a British cruiser." It was not desired to use force, but the presence of "the necessary force" with the food ships at Archangel would be "a powerful argument" to stop the stores leaving. Also 20 Royal Engineers would be on board the *Alexander*, "in the case necessity should arise for the destruction of the stores or of the railway in the event of emergency."[17] This minatory proposal did not shake Young.

He replied (March 20) that he considered the proposed proclamation "both undesirable and inexpedient", being likely to alienate the sympathy of the inhabitants. It would put them in the "impossible position of having to oppose the Central Government, on a question

16. F.O. 371, Vol. 3305, p. 188.

17. *Ibid.* pp. 253-255.

outside local competency, without any force behind them.", and would be likely to stimulate the Soviet Government Commission in Archangel to destroy the stores themselves if they could not remove them in time. In view of all this, he would assume the responsibility of not issuing the proclamation requested. Moreover, the very approach of war-ships escorting the convoy of food supplies might, once again, result in the destruction of the stores by the Commission "or by German agents". As for the sending of one icebreaker, even if armed, it would be insufficient to ensure reasonable hopes of success "under ice conditions, in view of the long distances to be covered in the river, and of the necessity of providing adequate guard for the stores pending their removal".[18]

On this despatch there was a revealing comment by a Foreign Office official. It said that the proposal had been made, not on the basis of information coming from Young, but of "a somewhat alarmist report produced by the Restriction of Enemy Supplies Department". All the other Foreign Office officials, up to and including Balfour himself, thereupon concurred in replying to Young that he could defer issuing the proclamation.

Young was obviously encouraged by this success to make a counter-proposal. He prepared an unofficial announcement to traders, which omitted the threats, underlined the food difficulties which Britain herself was experiencing, and announced the despatch of two food ships, given assistance by Russian icebreakers, "as an expression of good will towards the inhabitants of Archangel and of sympathy with them in their unfavourable position as regards essential foodstuffs". He also intended to distribute through the local post offices an anonymous statement to the same effect: and asked for Foreign Office approval (March 30, 1918).[19]

Once again, permission was given. The whole affair of the proposed proclamation brought out the sharp contrast between the "bull-at-the-gate" mentality in London, which was constantly obsessed with the vision of "standing no nonsense from the Bolsheviks" (not to speak of complete ignorance of political and even geographical conditions in Russia), and the careful and reasoned approach of Young — as loyal as ever, still as non-Bolshevik as any of his superiors, but well aware that the people of Russia (in this case, of Archangel) were in a mood not to be ignored.

He was obviously encouraged to press on still further with efforts to establish a more business-like climate for British-Soviet relations. On April 8, 1918, he sent a despatch which may be left to tell its own story.[20]

18. *Ibid.*, pp. 275-277.

19. *Ibid.*, pp. 316-317.

20. F.O. 371, vol. 3320, pp. 140-141.

"Crews of Russian ships requisitioned in the United Kingdom arrived here two weeks ago and have spread reports unfavourable to the British authorities. The substance of complaints is not so much the fact of requisition as that it was carried out in a manner calculated to offend their national feelings. They allege *inter alia*, that they were made to quit ship with insufficient notice, but could save all their belongings: that the Russian flag was ostentatiously replaced by the British under their eyes: and that they were marched off under armed guard and practically subjected to prisoner treatment until their departure. These statements which are reproduced in the press are so consistent as to indicate some foundation in fact. They have aroused a feeling of surprise and regret even in official circles friendly to us. I submit that however necessary and justifiable in principle these requisitions may be, they are most untimely in view of our weak position as regards war stores, etc. If they have been carried out in the clumsy and tactless manner alleged, it may be said without exaggeration that no better method could have been devised of impeding and counter-acting my efforts here to carry out your policy of creating in democratic circles a friendly feeling towards England. It is now unofficially reported that three Russian ships which left here in February last have also been requisitioned. In securing the departure of these ships I was largely instrumental, in conjunction with friendly local authorities, both acting in good faith. If these ships are now requisitioned, I as representative of His Majesty's Government will be open to suspicion of bad faith, and the local authorities who cooperated will be dangerously compromised with the Bolsheviks and exposed to the vengeance of the crews if and when the latter are sent back here".

This sensible appeal provoked a sour comment by another official, M.M. Knatchbull-Hughessen: "The majority of those who elect to return to Russia are Bolsheviks, which in itself explains much". Nevertheless he urged that everything should be done to avoid friction, and a reply was sent to Young that the Ministry of Shipping was going into the complaints.

On several other occasions Young showed his anxiety about the human problem created by the growing British hostility to the Soviet régime — though at that time he put them down to bureaucracy rather than to political prejudice. Thus on April 17 he asked about conditions in which visas could be granted to Russians and other foreigners wishing to come to Britain — possibly as refugees from Soviet Russia: and suggested that British subjects coming into Archangel from various parts of Russia should be taken directly on board ship, as the city was very much overcrowded (he estimated at

1200 — 1400 the number of Allied subjects wishing to leave). No visas could be granted to Russian subjects, he was told, and transport for the others was not yet available.[21] In May and June he had correspondence with the Foreign Office about 500 "Russian" miners brought from Lanarkshire in the autumn of 1917 (actually they must have been Lithuanians or Letts), and sent to Omsk. Now they had been returned to Archangel, unemployed, and there was a possibility of their being sent to their original homes in German-occupied territory. Young was against this, and secured agreement to their being retained at Archangel.[22]

On June 18 Young reported that the Central Jewish Refugee Committee at Petrograd were pressing him about a "considerable number" of wives and families stranded in Britain, after their breadwinners had been allowed to return to Russia in 1917. If this were true, he should be informed, as the Committee would have to make arrangements for their accommodation. He was told (July 2) that, while 192 women and children had been repatriated to Murmansk in April, the process was now "temporarily suspended". No reason was given, though before long it became obvious. In fact the files contain a memorandum from the Local Government Board (July 3) stating that 1,570 Russian women and 3,250 Russian children were now receiving public assistance, and that their repatriation was "desirable".[23]

5

By now London was pressing the question of the exchange of food supplies for the war stores — and therewith the possibility of persuading the Archangel authorities to break away from Moscow — more urgently than ever.

At first Young (April 12) repeated his previous warnings against giving "a handle for the accusation that we are directly prompting local opinion to act against the Central Authority", and stating that "there seems to be a strong feeling even amongst our friends that insistence on our part upon the return of all material e.g. metals and machine tools, urgently needed for Russian industries and especially

21. F.O. 371. vol. 3297, Foreign Office cable of May 8, 1918.
22. F.O. 371. vol. 3307, Young's despatches of May 6 and 29, 1918.
23. F.O. 371. vol. 3303.

railways, would be unfair, and that we ought to compromise on this point". Evidently sensing already that the British Supply Committee headed by General Poole had much more drastic actions in mind, Young added: "It would help me greatly if you could tell me confidentially how far His Majesty's Government propose to go to secure the war stores. I am assuming that" (*group indecipherable*) "sacrificed to the larger question of general economic relations". From the context, and bearing in mind Young's general attitude, it is most probable that the "indecipherable" words were something like "they may be".[24]

On April 15, reporting that the Archangel Soviet Executive Committee were against returning any of the war stores, "on the ground that these are essential to Russian industries and the revolutionary army", and that "there was no possibility of the stores falling into the hands of our enemies", Young added a significant paragraph: "They also hinted at the undesirability of any action on our part on the lines of recent events in the Far East" — a clear warning (for the first time) that forcible intervention such as that which had occurred at Vladivostok ten days before would be resisted. And he commented: "While I am inclined to believe in the sincerity of their desire to preserve the stores for Russia and not for Germany, the recent heavy despatch of metals (due doubtless to the involuntary disclosure of our deep interest in these by our agents somewhere) proves that the motive is not merely to preserve the stores from floods but also to forestall any attempt at seizure on our part. The choice of dumping-ground near Vologda, possessing rail and water communications in every direction, gives them the best available security in this respect and from the Germans at the same time".

Young further reminded his chiefs that the recent changes in the local administrative machinery had "strengthened Bolshevik control and correspondingly reduced the influence of the authorities friendly to us". (It will be remembered that the Archangel Soviet elections had reinforced Bolshevik representation and reduced the strength of the Socialist-Revolutionaries in the Regional Soviet). At the same time he believed that, if pressed, the Archangel Soviet "would go some way to meet us". But he submitted that "the use of force to secure a momentary interest may ruin the prospects of much greater advantages offered by the general economic question, which is already seriously held up by the conflict over stores". In view of the Soviet assurance, therefore, he suggested that — if the British Government were also prepared to compromise — "our face is saved by the non-publication of the conditions" (i.e. those laid down by the

---

24. F.O. 371. vol. 3305, pp. 398-399.

Foreign Office instructions about issuing a proclamation to the inhabitants).[25]

Following this up, Young reported (April 18) that the local Soviet was now "using its influence with the Central Authority to come to a speedy arrangement with us on the war stores question, on the ground of the economic advantages offered... They are also clearly influenced by fear of active interference on our part which they seem anxious to avoid at all costs". In view of this, Young urged, as he had done several times before, that the question of sending on food ships in order to take back stores had "lost its urgency".[26]

By April 29 the situation was becoming tense for other reasons. The President of the Archangel Regional Executive Committee (a Socialist-Revolutionary) had informed him confidentially that if Moscow did not agree to London's conditions about returning the stores, his Committee were prepared to satisfy those demands themselves, and even to declare their own "independence" on the lines he had reported in January. But evidently Young was not at all certain about the strength which his informant could command, and said it was desirable to give an assurance "that His Majesty's Government have no intention towards aggression or occupation of Russian territory... in order to strengthen the position of the pro-British majority".[27]

The Foreign Office replied with careful ambiguity (May 4). The British Commander at Murmansk (where by now there were 14,000 British, French and other Allied troops, and the local Soviet was openly defying the Soviet Government) had on April 25 declared publicly, by direction of the British Government, that the latter had not "and never have had any annexationist aims anywhere in Russia. This declaration applies to Archangel equally as to Murmansk. You may repeat this at Archangel". Young did so, in a letter to the City Soviet, and his statement was published in the local press. But the message he was directed to convey said nothing about occupation, as distinct from annexation. And, while stating that "non-intervention in the internal affairs of Russia" was still the British Government's policy, it was ready, Young was told, to render assistance "for the purpose of maintaining order", if the powers at the disposal of the local authorities — whom London regarded as a "properly constituted governing body for the district" — were insufficient for the task. Arrangements had already been made to send a British warship, *Attentive*, to Archangel, where she should arrive by the end of May.[28]

---

25. F.O. 371. vol. 3305, pp. 390-392.
26. *Ibid.*, pp. 401-402.
27. *Ibid.*, pp. 428-429.
28. *Ibid.*, p. 432.

Young, of course, would have been worse than incompetent if he had not understood this message as renewed encouragement to induce the Archangel Regional Committee to break away from its allegiance to the Soviet authorities, under the shelter of British armed forces which, without "occupying" Archangel, would help in "maintaining order" there!

A pungent comment on the whole business was made by Young himself, in the unpublished memoir which has been quoted previously. "The Bolsheviks certainly evacuated the stores from Archangel, and almost everything that was worth having was actually gone weeks before the occupation (August 2). But the real explanation of this evacuation, which was actually hastened by the threat of intervention, never seems to have occurred to the British authorities, so absorbed were they in looking for the hidden German hand. It never apparently occurred to them that, whilst they had jumped to the conclusion that the Bolsheviks intended to hand the stores over to the Germans, the Bolsheviks on their part with at least no less justification had made up their mind that the Allies intended to use them (as they eventually did use the remnant) to fight the Bolsheviks. That was made clear to any unbiassed mind on the spot by the place to which the stores were evacuated. They were dumped where the Allied diplomats had dumped themselves — at Vologda[29] — and for the very same reason, because it appeared to be the safest place from attack from any direction".

In fact, on May 14, Lenin gave Colonel Raymond Robins, who was leaving Moscow for the U.S.A., a "preliminary plan" of economic relations with America, which included the offer to guarantee that the war materials brought to Russia from Britain and the USA would not be sold to Germany.[30]

But by now there was a mass of evidence, available to Young and partly to the Soviet Government, that intervention against the Soviet authorities and occupation of Soviet territory by the Allies were developing in some areas and becoming an increasing possibility in others.

One was that Japanese military and naval forces had actually invaded Soviet territory at Vladivostok on April 5, 1918 — an act which could not have occurred without the active or passive consent of at least the British and French Governments. In fact, leading British Ministers had approved such intervention many weeks before, and had been pressing the United States to agree to it, as the Foreign Office files amply demonstrate.

---

29. At the end of February, 1918.

30. Quoted by G.F. Kennan, *The Decision to Intervene,* London, 1958, p. 219.

The second, equally public, were the murderous activities from January 8, 1918, onwards of the White Cossack bandit Semyonov, in Eastern Siberia, with open Japanese and more private Anglo-French support in arms and munitions — a form of indirect intervention.

A third, to which reference has aready been made, were the British and French activities in Murmansk. There had been a small naval and military mission there since 1916. In March, 1918, further landings of troops and arrival of Allied warships had at first been represented as aimed at warding off possible German/Finnish attack, and as such had been welcomed by the local Soviet (with a non-Bolshevik majority). Now they were developing into fully-fledged occupation, sanctioned by an ad hoc "Murmansk Regional Council" formed with the public approval of (and in fact by secret preliminary arrangement with) the Allied military and naval commanders on the spot.[31]

There were moreover smaller incidents. Thus, Young discovered that a man arriving from Petrograd with a British passport in the name of "Commander Thomson of the British Naval Mission" — a passport issued by the British Consul in Petrograd — was in reality a Russian officer, Captain Chaplin, who did not conceal from Young that his mission was to organise a White rising in Archangel to coincide with an Allied landing. At the end of May, Young also discovered that a member of General Poole's staff at Murmansk had been sent to Petrograd to get details of the counter-revolutionary White organisation there from the acting Naval Attaché, Captain Cromie, and had come to Archangel "with a sham appointment as a British Consular officer", to be joined shortly afterwards by Chaplin. From Poole himself, Young received a request (shortly after the General's arrival at Murmansk on May 24) to find billets at Archangel for 600 officers and men, "without exciting undue suspicion"— the request, coming to such a small a place as Archangel, "prompted one at first to suppose either that the General was a congenital idiot, or that he was under the very wrong impression that Russians were fools". In reality, the General sincerely believed "that he could walk ashore at Archangel with his gallant 600, ignore the Soviet authorities, and proceed with the raising and training of an anti-German Russian army".[32]

In Archangel itself, Young recorded, "the amazing indiscretions of the amateur Russian and Allied conspirators proclaimed almost from the housetops what was in the wind".

It will be necessary at this point to make a brief survey of what

---

31. The public side of this development had been advertised since mid-February in the Murmansk press, readily available in Archangel. The secret side is given by Kennan, *op. cit.*, pp. 114-117.

32. All these examples are taken from Young's unpublished memoir.

indeed "was in the wind", not only at Archangel but all over Russia — little of which was known to Young at the time.

This is the more important because for many years most histories of the invasion of Soviet Russia by Britain, France, Japan and the United States — an event which a whole generation of younger people today don't even know took place, incredible as this may seem — have been written by declared enemies of the Soviet Union, using documents drawn in the main from the archives of the United States. The USA were only gradually drawn into the invasion: they had to be persuaded, cajoled, even blackmailed into joining it. As consequence, the histories just mentioned have had the effect (whatever the intentions of their writers) of providing apologies for invasion, when they were not whitewashing it. Moreover, their efforts in turn had the result of pushing into the background the primary and inescapable responsibility of the then British Government for planning and promoting the attack on the Soviet Republic.

A striking and (I venture to say) honourable exception was the fourth volume of Mr Martin Gilbert's biography of Winston Churchill, published in 1975. His extracts from the papers of Churchill, Sir Henry Wilson (then Chief of the Imperial General Staff), the then British Commander-in-Chief Sir Douglas Haig and the British War Cabinet, in particular, showed up in great detail the relentless ferocity with which at first the whole British Government, and then Churchill and Wilson with some of their minor supporters, pursued the attempt to throttle the first Socialist Government in the world, even when Premier Lloyd George and Chancellor of the Exchequer Austen Chamberlain were losing their enthusiasm. I do not mean to say that in this Mr Gilbert was favourably inclined towards Soviet Russia, or even that he was impartial in his writing; but at least he was candid, unlike his predecessors in the field.

The chapter which follows seeks to place the responsibility for the invasion of 1918-1920 where it rightfully belongs, by examining the papers of the department which directly planned the attack, and with which Douglas Young himself had to contend.

PART II

6

On December 21, 1917, the British War Cabinet adopted on the proposal of Mr. A.J. Balfour, Foreign Secretary, the following memorandum (drafted by the Foreign Office) for submission to the French Government:

> "At Petrograd we should at once get into relations with the Bolsheviks through unofficial agents, each country as seems best to it.
>
> "We propose to send Sir George Buchanan on leave for reasons of health, but we shall keep a Chargé d'Affaires there. We do not suggest that our Allies should follow our example.
>
> "We should represent to the Bolsheviks that we have no desire to take part in any way in the internal politics of Russia, and that any idea that we favour a counter-revolution is a profound mistake. Such a policy might be attractive to the autocratic governments of Germany and Austria, but not to the Western democracies or America. But we feel it necessary to keep in touch so far as we can with the Ukraine, the Cossacks, Finland, Siberia, the Caucasus, etc. because these various semi-autonomous provinces represent a very large proportion of the strength of Russia. In particular, we feel bound to befriend the Ukraine, since upon the Ukraine depends the feeding of the Roumanians, to whom we are bound by every obligation of honour.
>
> "As for the War, we should carefully refrain from any word or action condoning the treachery of the Russians in opening peace negotiations with our enemies. But we should continually repeat our readiness to accept the principles of self-determination, and subject to that, of no annexations or indemnities. We should press on the Bolsheviks the importance of not being satisfied with empty phrases from the Germans, and point out that unless they get specific undertakings from them as to such questions as Poland, Bohemia, the Roumanian parts of Transylvania, not to speak of Alsace-Lorraine or the Trentino, they will get nothing. Meanwhile their powers of resistance are melting away, and they will soon be, if they are not now, at the mercy of the German Kaiser, who will then snap his fingers at all their fine phrases and impose on them any terms he pleases. They should be told that it is now probably too late to do anything to save the personnel of the Army. But the material of the artillery can still be preserved, and at the very least it should not be transferred to our enemies to be

used against the Western democracies. Most important of all, the Bolsheviks should prevent, if they can, the wheat districts of Russia, such as the Ukraine, falling into the control of, or being made available for, the Central Powers. This makes another reason why we are anxious to support and strengthen the Ukraine, and why we should urge on the Bolsheviks that, so far from trying to coerce the Ukrainians, they should enter into close cooperation with them.

"In Southern Russia our principal object must be, if we can, to save Roumania. Next we must aim at preventing Russian supplies from reaching Germany.

"Finally, we are bound to protect, if possible, the remnant of the Armenians, not only in order to safeguard the flank of our Mesopotamian forces in Persia and the Caucasus, but also because an Armenian, united if possible with the Georgian, autonomous or independent State, is the only barrier against the development of a Turanian movement that will extend from Constantinople to China, and will provide Germany with a weapon of even greater danger to the peace of the world than the control of the Baghdad Railway.

"If we could induce the Southern Russian armies to resume the fight, that would be very desirable, but it is probably impossible. To secure these objects, the first thing is money to reorganise the Ukraine, to pay the Cossacks and Caucasian forces, and to subsidise the Persians. The sums required are not, as things go, very enormous, but the exchange presents great difficulties. If the French would undertake the finance of the Ukraine, we might find the money for the others. It is understood that the United States will assist. Besides finance, it is important to have agents and officers to advise and support the provincial Governments and their armies. It is essential that this should be done as quietly as possible, so as to avoid the imputation — as far as we can — that we are preparing to make war on the Bolsheviks.

"We would suggest that the Ukraine should again, in this matter, be dealt with by the French, while we would take the other south-eastern provinces. A general officer from each country would be appointed to take charge of our respective activities, but they would of course keep in the closest touch with one another through carefully selected liaison officers, in order to ensure the utmost unity of action.

"It is for consideration whether we should facilitate the return to Southern Russia of the numerous Russian officers at present in France and England".

This memorandum was accepted by the French Premier Clémenceau and Foreign Minister Pichon two days later. The full text was first published by Prime Minister Lloyd George in his *War Memoirs* (Vol. II, ch. 71) in 1934.

On the same day the Allied representatives in Paris (who included on the British side Lord Robert Cecil, Under-Secretary for Foreign Affairs, and Lord Milner, Secretary for War) adopted a document dividing Russia into "zones" of their respective influence — Transcaucasia, North Caucasus, Central Asia and Northern Russia for Britain; Ukraine, Crimea and Bessarabia for France. A Foreign Office document of January 15, 1918 (F.O. 371, vol. 3314) put it more delicately — that the French would "occupy themselves with" Roumania and Ukraine, while the British would "look after" the Caucasus, etc.

Political assurances that the British Government favoured self-determination were hardly likely to persuade the Bolsheviks, coming from a Government which at that time maintained military rule over India, Egypt and Ireland. Similarly, good advice as to how to protect Russia from the Germans was most unlikely to take the British Government very far. What was really significant about the remarkable Balfour memorandum was, that while disavowing any support of counter-revolution, it proposed to give financial and military support, all over Russia, to none other than counter-revolutionaries. It would indeed be underestimating the intelligence of the British Foreign Secretary and his diplomatic advisers, as well as of the British military agents in Russia, to suppose that they did not understand that counter-revolutionaries — both Tsarist and bourgeois — would willingly proclaim themselves "anti-German" if this meant that they would get material help from Britain and her allies against the Bolsheviks. And this in fact is what happened.

The Balfour memorandum of December, 1917 — six weeks after the October Revolution — was in fact a master-plan for anti-Soviet intervention and counter-revolution. The whole course of events thereafter demonstrated this — which is hardly surprising, seeing that the Ministers in charge of the armed forces and the secret services, no less than those heading the Foreign Office, took part in adopting the memorandum. Whichever of the "provincial governments and their armies", during the next three years, received the Allied help decided on (at first financial, later consisting of guns, tanks and munitions) — and whatever their title — over the vast mosaic represented by Russia in the civil war years, they were in fact anti-Bolshevik.

The memorandum itself had its pre-history. A Foreign Office paper by Lord Robert Cecil, dated February 23, 1918, recorded that "at the end of November (1917) the Cabinet began to consider how far it would support movements which were anti-Bolshevik and pro-Entente, and after some hesitation decided to provide money for such movements". Referring to the subsequent decisions of December 23, Lord Robert noted that "it was distinctly agreed that if the result of such action was to produce a rupture with the Bolsheviks, we should not be deterred by that happening". Moreover, on December 3, 1917 — three weeks *before* the Balfour memorandum — the War Cabinet instructed Lord Robert Cecil to inform Sir George Buchanan the British Ambassador in Petrograd, that "the policy of the Government is to support any responsible body in Russia which would actively oppose the Maximalists, and that H.M. Government would give money freely to those who proved ready to support the Allied cause".[33] It mentioned in particular such aid to the Cossacks and the Ukrainians.

Writing in the decent obscurity of a Foreign Office minute, Cecil did not resort to the subterfuge of calling the movements "anti-German": giving a spade its legitimate title of spade, he called them "anti-Bolshevik", as did the War Cabinet.

Another War Cabinet minute, no. 298 of December 14, 1917, ordered that "any money required for the purpose of maintaining alive in South East Russia the resistance to the Central Powers" i.e. to the Bolsheviks, was to be paid, if it was "considered necessary by the War Office in consultation with the Foreign Office".

Moreover, a joint note of the military representatives attending the Supreme War Council of the Allies in Paris recorded on December 24, 1917, that they had been asked — on the initiative of the British Government — to give their opinion as to whether Southern Russia and Roumania were able "to resist the Bolshevik forces assisted and controlled by the Germans". This was — as a far from pro-Soviet historian has pointed out — one of the earliest statements which "assumed that the Allies were fighting Bolsheviks as well as Germans".[34]

However, the practical effect of applying the Balfour memorandum would be even more striking: the Allied forces would be fighting the Bolsheviks in regions where the Germans were never

---

33. F.O. 371, vol. 3290; and War Cabinet Minute 289[2]. "Maximalists" was a term freely applied in these first months to the Bolsheviks.

34. Ullman, *Intervention and the War* (London 1961) p. 56. It is indeed surprising that Mr. Kennan (*Russia Leaves the War,* 1956, pp. 178-179) while giving extracts from the Balfour Memorandum, omits the whole sentence about sending the officers "as quietly as possible", etc. Mr. Ullman's text alters "quietly" to "quickly", thereby totally changing the meaning; and Mr. Silverlight *(The Victors' Dilemma,* 1970), overlooks not only the tell-tale sentence, but the whole preceding passage! Mr. Swettenham *Allied Intervention in Russia, 1918-1919,* London, 1967) does not even mention the Balfour Memorandum.

seen, being thousands of miles away. And events immediately began to demonstrate this quite conclusively.

7

A number of books have been written on the history of Allied intervention in Russia in 1918-1920 as a whole — some by British, American and French authors, others in the Soviet Union. The present chapter will be confined to the question only of the initial stages of several invasions and interventions, as revealed (primarily) in the British archives.

Kaledin. This Cossack general, commanding troops at Novocherkassk, had on November 7, 1917, publicly denounced the Soviet Government and proclaimed that he was assuming "full State power" in the Don Region; and on November 13 he ordered one of his divisions to attack the Bolsheviks at Voronezh. Although he was foiled in this attempt, he took steps to consolidate his authority, declaring a state of war, in the Donetz coal-field first of all, and then throughout the Don Cossack Region. After heavy fighting his forces occupied Rostov on December 15 and, soon after, the southern half of the Donetz coal-field. Well-known Tsarist generals like Alexeyev, Kornilov and Denikin, politicians like the Cadet Miliukov, the former right-wing Duma President Rodzianko and the Socialist-Revolutionary Savinkov, joined Kaledin, and began helping in the formation of a White "Volunteer Army". Every success of theirs in the coalfield was attended by massacres of miners.[35]

On November 22, 1917, Balfour had instructed the British Minister at Jassy, on the Roumanian-Russian border, to send an agent to Kaledin to enquire if he would support the Roumanian army against the Bolsheviks. (This was on the direct instructions of the War Cabinet, as its minute no. 280, the same day, shows). A British officer stationed at Tiflis was sent on the orders of the British Ambassador at Petrograd on November 30 to the Don for the same purpose. On December 1, the British, French and Italian Premiers, meeting in Paris, had resolved to send to Kaledin a combined Anglo-French military mission. On December 3 the British War Cabinet decided to guarantee to Kaledin all the financial support he needed: and on the same day the Chief of the Imperial General Staff cabled

35. Mintz, *op. cit.*, vol. III (1973) pp. 126-127, 489, 497-500.

accordingly to the British Military Attaché in Jassy that he could "grant Kaledin financial support up to any figure necessary". Despite later information from Buchanan about the doubtful nature of the support commanded by Kaledin, the War Cabinet had by December 14 approved a first payment to Kaledin of £10 millions.[36]

This intervention in support of the most prominent of the anti-Bolshevik military forces had actually begun *before* the Anglo-French agreements of December 23 and 24, 1917.

Aid in this region to the Whites thereafter developed rapidly. A cable from Lord Bertie, British Ambassador in Paris, on January 3 1918, reported that the French Government was giving Alexeyev, Kaledin's commander-in-chief, 100 million francs: and on January 10, 1918, a British major in Kiev reported to the British military attaché at Jassy that he had arranged with Alexeyev's representative there to pay him 10,000 roubles a week "to pass selected officers through the Don to join Alexeyev".[37]

This financial intervention, later backed with weapons, munitions and even uniforms, was not to end until Wrangel's forces were driven from the Crimea three years later, after great loss of life and destruction of property all over south Russia.

Siberia. On January 1, 1918, after a discussion in the War Cabinet about more than 600,000 tons of war stores at Vladivostok which had been supplied by the U.S.A. and Britain on credit, and also about the possibility of the Japanese themselves occupying and exploiting Eastern Siberia, it was decided to send a British cruiser from Hong Kong to Vladivostok, and to place two infantry companies in readiness to go there as well. This naturally prompted the Japanese, when they were informed, to do the same — and they anticipated the British, being closer at hand. Their warship arrived on January 12 and the British cruiser on the 14th. An American warship followed on March 11. This was the beginning of many months of discussions between the Allies as to whether a joint military expedition of British, American, French, Japanese and Chinese troops should occupy the Russian Far Eastern Maritime Provinces starting from Manchuria (as the French had proposed on January 7, 1918); or whether the Japanese should occupy the whole Trans-Siberian Railway on behalf of the Allies (as the British proposed on January 28): or whether they should occupy only the eastern section of the Railway (as the Japanese offered to do on February 8). All these questions, examined at considerable length by the American historians of intervention, are really irrelevant to the main point — that the British Government *on its own*, and in complete accord with

36. Ullman, *op. cit.*, pp. 43, 48, 52.

37. F.O. 371, vol. 3283.

the terms of the Balfour Memorandum of December 21, 1917, had ten days after that paper set the example of foreign invasion of the Russian Far East — at a time when Soviet power had been established from one end of Siberia to the other.[38]

And this started the process which led to the large-scale Japanese landing on April 5, 1918: the formation (with varied financial and military support from the Allies) of a series of local "governments" in Siberia — at loggerheads with one another, but all fighting the Bolsheviks and overthrowing the local Soviets, with large-scale massacre wherever they gained power: and the ultimate establishment at Omsk in November, 1918, of the Kolchak military dictatorship which ruled Siberia for a number of months.

Meanwhile, on January 6, 1918, the Foreign Office in a circular to the British Ambassadors in Paris, Rome, Washington and Tokyo[39] had informed them that Col. Josiah Wedgwood was being sent to Siberia "to make clear to the whole of Siberia" the anti-German purposes of the Allies, and their readiness to support, encourage and assist elements "which continue to resist by all means in their power German tendencies and German power". This was the propaganda aspect, as it were, of putting into effect the Balfour Memorandum — since by now it was generally accepted that "German" in official British terminology meant "Bolshevik", especially in Siberia where there were no Germans within thousands of miles — except prisoners of war!

It is not without interest, too, in this connection that a memorandum of January 19, 1918, from the Inter-Departmental Committee which met daily at the Foreign Office, and which (as Balfour minuted) had been devised jointly by the War Office and the Foreign Office — the document was circulated to the King and the War Cabinet — began by asserting the importance of Japanese intervention in Siberia, "to prevent it becoming a German preserve", but went on to argue that becoming "masters of Siberia" was the only way by which the Allies could keep the necessary supply of munitions and material going "to the anti-Bolshevik elements" in Southern Russia. Even earlier, there was a Foreign Office cable to the Consul at Odessa on January 11, 1918, reporting discussion with the Japanese as to the methods of intervention to control the Trans-Siberian Railway, precisely for the purpose mentioned in the memorandum of January 19. Obviously it was an uneasy conscience that led a Foreign Office functionary to append his comment (January 16) to the first draft of the Inter-Departmental Committee's memorandum: that intervention would certainly be welcomed by

38. Ullman *op. cit.*, pp. 90-93, 102.

39. F.O. 371, vol. 3297.

"the landed proprietors, industrial magnates, Cossack leaders, etc." But he had doubts about "the real feelings of the mass of the people". Might they not think that intervention was being "undertaken with the object of surpressing Bolshevism?". Large areas of Russia had decided that Bolshevism was "a desirable form of government". There might be a very serious humanitarian-pacifist-international syndicalist agitation, "if we try by armed force to convince them that it isn't".[40]

However, the doubts of this prescient official were ignored, and large-scale intervention was the outcome of British initiative here too.

Semyonov. This captain in the Tsarist army had been sent in September, 1917, to the Far East by the Council of the Union of Cossack Forces to combat Bolshevik influences among the Cossack of that region. This of course was before the October Revolution. The Chinese seizure of the railway running through that area, linking Central Siberia with the Far-Eastern provinces (December 16, 1917) enabled Semyonov to begin forming a "Special Manchurian Force" at Harbin, in Manchuria. The "Force" was composed of some Russian officers, about 150 Cossacks and some 400 Chinese professional bandits, most of them from the Chinese side of the border. At the beginning of January, 1918, in a night raid, he seized the frontier railway station of Manchuria and shot the members of the local Soviet, terrorising the soldiers on guard duty into joining his detachment. Following this success, he captured a number of other stations, thereby cutting the railway communications. Massacres, floggings and plunder accompanied Semyonov's operations throughout. A note from the British Chargé d'Affaires in Washington to the U.S. Secretary of State reported that, given Allied support in arms, munitions and money, Semyonov planned to take Chita, Irkutsk and Krasnoyarsk, as a preliminary to seizing the whole Trans-Siberian line and thereafter, as he hoped, breaking through westwards in order to join forces with the Cossacks of Orenburg in the southern Urals, under Dutov, and Kaledin's Cossacks on the Don.[41]

From the outset Semyonov presented a great attraction for the Allies, but particularly for the British Government and the Japanese. On January 28, 1918, the British Military Attaché at Peking reported that he had received Semyonov's representative, while his assistant had met Semyonov himself and was impressed by his "soldierly

40. The document of January, 19, 1918, is in F.O. 371, vol. 3296. The cable of January 11, 1918 with appended comments is in F.O. 371, vol. 3288.

41. The note is quoted from the U.S. Documents on Foreign Policy by Mintz, *op.cit.*, pp. 696-697.

qualities". He recommended meeting Semyonov's demands — guns, shells, machine-guns, a couple of armoured cars, and £10,000 a month to pay new recruits, who would bring his strength up to 3,000 men — as "practical". Balfour on February 2, 1918, in a note to the State Department, endorsed this scheme, because it was "of the greatest importance to support purely Russian movements in Siberia". Britain had told Semyonov through her Consul at Harbin that she would support him with money and arms, and Balfour hoped that the U.S.A. would do the same.[42] The Japanese already had a liaison officer with Semyonov.

Furthermore, the Foreign Office had already instructed its Consul at Vladivostok on January 31, 1918, that if Russian officers offered their services, he should advise them "to join Semyonov or other operations of a similar nature".[43] On February 27 the British Minister at Peking reported to the Foreign Office that the Consul at Harbin had by the 23rd paid Semyonov £2,000 through his "Russian" (Tsarist) colleague, and would advance a second sum of £10,000 — "or further sums" — if his movement progressed. On March 7 the Minister further reported that he was handing over to the "Russian Legation", for Semyonov, two howitzers and 800 rounds from the arsenal of the Peking Legation Quarter, and that an artillery N.C.O. was being sent with these arms as instructor, and also an officer in plain clothes.[44] At the same time the Japanese were supplying Semyonov with field guns, machine-guns and 22 gunners. In April the assistant British Military Attaché in Peking was sent to inspect the "Special Manchurian Force".

By this time Lockhart, the British unofficial agent in Moscow, was protesting against the Allies' support of Semyonov, which was making his relations with the Soviet authorities difficult; and in a comment on a further despatch from Peking, Sir Ronald Graham minuted at the Foreign Office (April 6): "It is clear that Mr. Lockhart was justified in describing Semyonov's force as composed of Chinese brigands and as being counter-revolutionary".

Lockhart was probably aware of the report by Col. Wedgwood that, as he had learned in February in Tokyo, "Semyonov's methods are loot and terrorism... He harms the Allied cause in Siberia and Russia".[45]

But when a message from Lockhart reported that one of his staff,

---

42. Ullman, *op. cit.*, pp. 99-100, quoting from *Foreign Relations of the United States, 1918, Russia,* vol. II, pp. 38-41.

43. F.O. 371, vol. 3296.

44. F.O. 371, vol. 3289.

45. F.O. 371, vol. 3297. Wedgwood's report is attached to a communication from the Director of Military Intelligence much later (May 8).

Capt. Hicks, was attending a Soviet-Chinese conference at Chita about Semyonov's depredations, the Far Eastern Department of the Foreign Office, evidently in some displeasure, minuted (April 8): "We are rightly or wrongly supporting Semyonov, and Capt. Hicks is well aware of the fact. He is nevertheless apparently to take part in a conference the object of which is to break up Semyonov's organisation". However, in fact the financing of the bandit leader continued.[46]

Before long the Semyonov affair was fully merged in the larger intervention which the Western Allies had already begun to establish together with the Japanese. Here it is sufficient to underline that this is a further example of the truth that the choice of Semyonov as a means of "quietly" promoting counter-revolution in one corner of Russia was not accidental. It followed directly from the Cabinet decisions of December 21, 1917.

Transcaucasia. A well-known *Times* correspondent in Russia, H.R. Wilton, had in January, 1918, suggested to the French Foreign Minister Pichon that Allied agents should be sent into Central Asia to combat the "German" i.e. Bolshevik influence. On an enquiry about this from Pichon, Balfour replied to the French Ambassador in London, Cambon, (January 30, 1918) that "steps are already being taken by the Government of India to organise a mission which could, in case of emergency, proceed to Turkestan and enter into relations with anti-Bolshevik elements in that region". In fact, on January 18 the Army Council had told the India Office that it agreed to the preparation of a "suitable mission" in which the officers "should be men of initiative and enterprise, and should be kept plentifully supplied with funds". Captain P.T. Etherton was available for this purpose. Selected officers should be sent to Kashgar (in Chinese Turkestan) and Meshed (in Northern Persia) "without further delay", wrote Balfour on March 29, 1918. In fact (an Army Council letter of June 14, 1918, told the Foreign Office) a British General Staff officer, Lieut.-Col. E. A. F. Redl, had been sent to Meshed — actually he was there early in April — to be in charge of an Intelligence Mission in the town. His instructions (issued on May 13 by the British Commander-in-Chief in India) included demolitions on the Transcaspian Railway, in the event of a "Turkish or German advance" to that region.[47]

But Balfour's communication to Cambon of January 30 shows that, here as elsewhere, the reference to Germans or Turks was merely the standard formula covering the anti-Bolshevik purposes of the inter-

46. F.O. 371, vol. 3290.

47. All these papers, beginning with Balfour's letter of January 30, are collected in F.O. 371. vol. 3303.

ventionist plans. And it is not without interest that an Australian infantry officer, Col. C.H. Ellis, who was appointed in July, 1918, to a military mission sent to Meshed soon after the Redl mission, wrote many years afterwards that the military mission had already made contact "with anti-Bolshevik rebels against a Soviet Government at Tashkent, and a relationship with them was growing up that was to lead to British and Indian troops being involved in military operations against Bolshevik troops along the Central Asian Railway".[48]

It would be again straining credulity beyond endurance to expect anyone to believe that the instructions sanctioned by Balfour on January 30, and obviously guiding Redl's activities at Meshed in the spring, did not apply to the military mission (commanded by General Malleson) which arrived there in June. Yet it was the work of that mission, as military writers like Generals Dunsterville and Malleson, Colonel Ellis and others have shown, which began the larger intervention of British forces in Transcaucasia and Transcaspia and their support of the White régimes in those regions. A report to the War Office from the Commander-in-Chief, India, on the recent activities in Baku of one of the mission's agents, Capt. Teague-Jones, stated in characteristic language on July 27, 1918: "The Baku Bolsheviks are almost certainly in enemy pay, and would obstruct as much as possible active British intervention. But their position is insecure, and their fate would almost certainly be precipitated by active measures by us".[49]

Turkestan. As for Capt. (later Lt.-Col.) Etherton, he himself described in after years how he was sent to Kashgar (in Sinkiang province, near the Russian frontier) under instructions, the language of which was obviously copied direct from the Army Council decision of January 18. But he developed it in the following terms: "Although it was not contemplated to afford effective military support to pro-Allied elements, a small British military organisation was essential, from which the antennae could radiate for the acquisition of information, and to exploit whatever appeared to be favourable". One of the "antennae" was his own appointment as British Consul-General and Political Resident at Kashgar, where the mission (which had already begun to assemble in April) arrived on July 7, 1918. Other "antennae" were two other experienced officers of the Indian Army, Col. Bailey and Major Blacker, who had to go to Tashkent, centre of Soviet power in Central Asia, "to investigate the situation on the spot, and examine questions affecting the safety and welfare of

---

48. *The Trans-Caspian Episode* (London 1963), pp. 14-15.

49 F.O. 371, vol. 3335 (July 26) and vol. 3300 (July 27).

the British Empire".

Col. Bailey soon discovered that this kind of language could not throw his hosts, the Soviet authorities at Tashkent, off the scent. He was asked on his arrival there (August 14, 1918) "to explain why a friendly mission should come to them from Kashgar, whilst from the direction of Persia and Askabad in the west British troops should be attacking the Bolsheviks and taking possession of the country. It was indeed hard to reconcile these two lines of action". Sir George Macartney, Etherton's predecessor at Kashgar, supplied the standard explanation — that the British presence "was dictated by strategical reasons arising out of the war against Germany". Naturally, this did not satisfy the Soviet leaders.[50] Bailey's subsequent activities — at the time when there was a White Cossack revolt in western Turkestan — included going into hiding for over a year, and during this time maintaining contact with agents of the anti-Bolshevik Whites: these were described later in his own book.[51]

Col. Etherton, soon after his arrival at Kashgar, established "cordial relations" with the former Tsarist Consul-General Uspensky, who had rejected relations with the Soviet Government. To Uspensky he owned "much of the success that attended my efforts to fight the insidious disease of Bolshevism". What were these efforts? He gave a general indication of these in his reference to the difficulties encountered by the Soviet authorities at Tashkent — "confronted by the British in north-east Persia, and meeting with strong opposition from insurgent bands in Semirechia and Ferghana, *with all of whom I was in touch*". What "in touch" meant — at the time when British sterling and British arms were being supplied to anti-Soviet forces all round the Soviet borders — awaits more detailed study of the archives. But when Etherton, investigating the activities of Indians engaged in gun-running through Kashgar to Afghanistan, uncovered one such case, "the man declared that the arms were intended only for sale to the insurgents of Ferghana, who were in arms against the Bolsheviks, a statement I was inclined to believe". So he sent the offender back to India instead of having him arrested.[52]

50. P.T. Etherton, *In the Heart of Asia* (London, 1925) pp. 5, 7, 10, 96-97.

51. F.M. Bailey, *Mission to Tashkent,* (London, 1946).

52. Etherton, *op. cit.* pp.110, 151, 215, 270,-272.

8

Another aspect of how intervention — on the surface only the result of chance circumstances, but in reality started on the direct initiative of the Allies (and particularly Britain) — is of exceptional importance, since it bears on Allied activity in the very heart of Soviet Russia.

The master-plan for intervention laid down on December 21, 1917, plays the same part as elsewhere for the most serious threat which faced the Soviet Republic within its first year of existence. This threat was the mutiny, or rebellion, or rising (whichever name may be preferred) of the Czechoslovak Legion in May, 1918, formed out of prisoners of Czech and Slovak nationality taken from the Austro-Hungarian Army. Its fifty to seventy thousand men (the figures depend upon the exact dates chosen) were well armed, disciplined and organised, and strung out along the main railways from southern Russia to Omsk in Siberia. They had in most of their principal units, in positions of command, Russian Tsarist officers, appointed in the course of 1917. These officers "were to a man anti-Communist. To some extent, they were in touch with underground Russian opposition groups" — in plain language, with counter-revolutionaries.[53] To have this force turn actively against the Soviets, at a time when the Red Army was only in process of formation, was a deadly menace just because it was installed in the very heart of the country. For that very reason, the Allies were particularly interested in it from the very start — though it was not so directly accessible to them as the potential White forces in the border-lands of the former Russian Empire and therefore it took longer to bring into action.

But the process began at once. At a meeting of Allied military representatives at Jassy at the end of November, 1917, Vaclav Čeržensky, the delegate of the Czechoslovak Legion in Roumania, was asked whether the Legion was in a position to attack the Bolsheviks with the object of occupying the Ukraine. He replied that this was possible, providing it received adequate support in war material from the Allies.[54] Years later, President Masaryk confirmed this in essence. Pressure was put on the Czechoslovaks, he said, to

54. Quoted from the published report by Smeral, "Czechoslavaks and SR's", Moscow, 1922.

53. Kennan, *op. cit.* p.143.

place themselves at the disposal of the Allies in Russia, rather than go to France. *"London would rather have seen us stay in Russia or Siberia"*. But he too "had thought much on the subject of war against the Bolshevists and Russia, and I would have attached our Corps to any army strong enough to fight the Bolshevists and the Germans in the name of democracy". In practice, he thought, only intervention by the Japanese could make this possible. In any case, he wrote, it was not practicable "to occupy and hold the immense territory of European Russia with 50,000 men. We should have had to occupy Kiev and a large number of towns and villages in the direction of Moscow, leaving garrisons everywhere — an enterprise entirely beyond our strength".[55] The reason for his reference to Kiev will appear later.

However, what the Czech leaders did do in November, 1917, on the evidence of a former Legionary, Kurfürst, who handed in his recollections to President Masaryk's Chancery (January 28, 1927) was — with Masaryk's consent — to allow Legionaries of the 2nd Regiment stationed at Kiev to slip away to the Don, in order to take service in General Kornilov's counter-revolutionary Cossack forces then being organised. The Czechs were allowed to form a detachment of their own, under Engineer Král, and to take in individual unattached Czechs coming from various parts of Russia.[56]

Meanwhile, the Allied military authorities had not abandoned the idea put to the Legion's representative at Jassy. On December 7, 1917 — still before the Balfour Memorandum — the French Foreign Minister wrote to Eduard Benes — Masaryk's colleague in the leadership of the Czech National Council formed in exile — inviting him and their third colleague Stefanik to join a "Commission for the Settlement of the Russian Question", which had been formed at the French Ministry of Foreign Affairs under General Janin, who had been France's representative at the Russian High Command during the Tsarist régime. The object of this Commission was to "prepare a plan of propaganda and a plan of action, and to study the possibility of the fullest use of some organisations of foreigners in Russia, for example the Czechs, Cossacks etc." [57] The deliberately general terms of the letter hardly needs decyphering, bearing in mind that the French were already helping materially in the formation of the Cossack anti-Soviet army at Novocherkassk on the Don, under Kaledin and Kornilov.

55.. *The Making of a State* (translation of "Svetová Revoluce"), London 1927, pp. 182-184.

56. Archives of the President's Military Chancery, (Prague), T4 V.K., 1927.

57. Archives of the Institute of Military History, Prague/VHA, fond Ceskoslovenská národní rada v Parizi (CSNR/1917 sign. 6/4/10).

In this — as might have been expected after the discussions at Jassy — Britain was not far behind. Major J.K.L. Fitzwilliams — the officer sent to interview Kaledin at Novocherkassk by the British Military Attaché at Jassy — reported to the latter on December 12 that he considered "the Czech organisation the best and the most likely to lead to the possible formation of a strong government" (in Russia). It possessed two well-equipped and well-disciplined divisions, "which is more than any other party can claim". If the Allies were willing to risk the money, he thought that within six months "a force of half-a million troops could be collected and armed". The results would be "invaluable".[58] Then, on December 16, 1917, the French Government recognised the Czech Legion in Russia as an autonomous part of the Czechoslovak Army in France — which was under the general direction of the French High Command. The presumption was that it would be evacuated to France through the Far East. But in fact influences tending to another direction began to be exercised before long.

So far as Masaryk was concerned, the most revealing record is that of his conversations in Moscow with Boris Savinkov, the Socialist-Revolutionary terrorist and organiser of anti-Bolshevik insurrections, on March 2 and 5, 1918. The notes, in his own hand, are fragmentary but sufficiently eloquent. They read:

"I — my opinion.
He will negotiate with Klecanda, Maxa.
I — that he should: A. buy up grain, lest it go to Germans. With textiles!...
B. If necessary, "grain terror".
C. Polit. terror?
Alexeyev writes that he isn't crushed, retiring southward.
Terror: assassination of Grand Duke Sergei cost only 7,000 rbls. Plehve — 30,000.
I can provide some financial resources.
— to Shiep, that Klecanda 200,000 rbls".[59]

---

58. F.O. 371, vol. 3314, pp. 275-6.

59. Masaryk Archives, Russia 1918 (Prague). Klecanda was secretary of the Czech National Council in Moscow, Maxa its vice-president. Textiles were mentioned because the peasants would part with their grain most readily for such goods. The Grand Duke was assassinated by a Socialist-Revolutionary in February, 1905; Plehve, Minister of the Interior, also by a Socialist-Revolutionary in July, 1904. Schiep held the finances of the National Council. In his memoirs *(op. cit.,* p. 189), Masaryk of course wrote much more vaguely — and indeed quite misleadingly — of these conversations, not mentioning the financial aid he offered Savinkov. But some points in his notes, e.g. about offering goods to the peasants in exchange for grain, were later repeated in Masaryk's memorandum to President Wilson on April 10, 1918, *(op. cit.* p.193).

At the same time British pressure to use the Legion for counter-revolution in Russia, rather than let it go to France, was resumed in a bigger way. On March 18 Consul-General Wardop cabled from Moscow to London that the Czech representatives had informed him of the impending departure of 70,000 Czechs from Kursk for France via Vladivostok. The War Office suggested to the Foreign Office (March 30) that "it would seem far wiser to allow them to remain in Russia where their presence might be of importance". It suggested three different ways in which they could be used (i) at Omsk, to reinforce the 2nd Corps which the Czech National Council was forming, or (ii) at Archangel, "to protect stores in that port, and perhaps keep open communications with Siberia through Perm, though it seems incredible that it would be allowed to do so", or (iii) in Transbaikalia to cooperate with Semyonov: "the last seems the most feasible".[60] The same proposal was made by the War Office next day to the Czechoslovak National Council, through the French Government.[61]

Meanwhile, the ground had been well prepared with the Czechoslovak National Council in Moscow. On March 31, 1918, Klecanda wrote secretly to the representatives of the Council near Penza, where there was a large group of Czechoslovak soldiers. "I am writing to you only for information, insisting on complete secrecy", he said, proceeding to tell them that a coup d'état was expected in the immediate future. It would establish a coalition government of Mensheviks, Socialist-Revolutionaries "and such-like", without extremist parties, either right or left. But it would have a pro-Ally programme, and there would be efforts to unite with the left-wing Cadets. What this would mean politically he indicated too: "The SRs are ready to give up the idea of a republic for concessions in the programme, for the sole purpose of preserving the honour and strength of Russia". The alliance with the Cadets would make success much more probable. "In the event of reconstruction of the government in the interests of the Allies, it will be necessary, if possible, to leave appropriate cadres of the I Corps here for further formations, and thus help the new government. In that event the presence of our armed forces in Siberia" (i.e. the II Corps forming at Omsk) "would play an important part. The only thing is, not to disarm. Tomorrow I will go to the British to find out how matters stand with a British landing at Archangel, and whether they intend actively or passively to support the possible reconstruction of the government". Masaryk, in

60. See chapter 7 for this bandit leader.

61. F.O. 371, vol. 3323; and Benes, *Souvenirs de Guerre et de Révolution,* (Paris, 1929), t. II, pp. 184-185.

his memoirs, also wrote in general terms that just before he left Moscow on March 7, 1918, "there was talk of an offensive on the part of the Socialist-Revolutionary element in the Moscow Bolshevist administration" and that Klecanda was given "full powers to conduct political negotiations".[62]

Obviously the meeting between Masaryk and Savinkov at the beginning of March had not been the only one of its kind. Obviously, too, the question of evacuating the Legion overseas had, for the Czechoslovak National Council, become purely academic: both Corps of the Legion were to be used in Russia, as British officials had suggested, in the event of the"reconstruction of the government" i.e. of a coup d'état.

The reference to not disarming was no less significant. Only four days before the letter was written, on March 27, 1918, an agreement had been signed at Penza by Soviet representatives on the instructions of the Soviet Government and by representatives of the Legion. By this agreement, most of the counter-revolutionary Russian officers were to be dismissed, the Czechoslovak troops were to proceed unhindered to Vladivostok, and they were to retain only such arms as were essential for defence against counter-revolutionaries.[63] The arms concerned, by an agreement arrived at the previous day in Moscow, were to consist of 168 rifles and one machine-gun per echelon, with 300 rounds per rifle and 1200 rounds per machine-gun.[64]

But in reality the Czech troops did not surrender all the arms required by the agreement: considerable quantities were retained and concealed in the trains. The branch of the National Council at Penza was well aware of this, and "tacitly approved".[65]

On April 4-5 the Japanese landed in force at Vladivostok. This changed the whole situation. There was now in being the intervention by a major Power which Masaryk had conceived of, six months before, as the essential condition for the Czechoslovak forces intervening in their turn against the Bolsheviks: moreover it was the very state which Masaryk had had in mind. From that time onwards, while there was argument between the British, sticking to their proposals to use the Legion in Russia, and the French, who formally persisted in their demand for shipping it to France, the destiny of the Legion in the immediate future — to attack the Bolsheviks as part of the general Allied plan — was decided. Immediately following events

62. VHA. OCSNR/pres/1918/cj 5206 (Prague); and Masaryk, *op. cit.*, pp. 188-189.

63. Kennan, *op.cit.*, p. 142.

64. *Istoricheski Zhurnal* (Moscow), No. 12, 1940, p. 48.

65. Benes, *op.cit.*, pp. 180, 197.

made this clear.

On April 8 the Allied military representatives in Paris, apart from the Americans, approved a British staff paper providing in effect that "the Czechs would form part of a future Allied force in Siberia".[66] On April 13, in a secret council of war held by the officers of the first Czech division, it was decided not to surrender the surplus arms, and if necessary to fight their way through the east "otherwise than by negotiations". This decision was kept a secret from the soldiers.[67] But it fitted into all the previous proceedings like a piece in a jigsaw puzzle — as did the next events.

On April 15 Lockhart cabled from Moscow that, according to the Vice-President of the Czechoslovak National Council, the 60,000 men by now at Omsk might be detained "if the Allies take action in the Far East", and in that case would make for Archangel. On April 17 — not yet having received Lockhart's cable — the War Cabinet discussed the use of the Czech Corps. Balfour pointed out that the question was now part of "the general situation as to Russia and intervention by the Allies as a whole via Siberia". He suggested trying to persuade the Soviet authorities to allow the Czechs to come to Archangel or Murmansk "with a view to preventing encroachments in Russia by the forces of the Central Powers": and was authorised to cable Lockhart to this effect. (It is noteworthy that Balfour was making the same suggestion as the Czech officials were making to Lockhart in Moscow). Two days later, the Chief of the Imperial General Staff advised against this formula: it would be better to ask the Soviet Government "to facilitate their journey to Murmansk or Archangel in order that they may be shipped from there to France". Nevertheless, on April 20 the cable went to Lockhart as originally formulated.[68]

The reason for not accepting the suggestion of the C.I.G.S. was clear. The Soviet Government knew, just as well as the British, that there was neither the shipping nor any other essential condition to make possible evacuation from Archangel. This was why, on the Allies pressing their suggestion, Lenin asked a month later for guarantees that the evacuation would be immediate i.e. that the Czechs would be put on board directly they arrived. The device had failed to take in the Soviet Government.[69]

On the other hand, the terms used in Balfour's cable of April 20, to the effect that the transfer of the Czechs to North Russia was for the

66. Ullman, *op.cit.*, p. 154, quotes the minutes from the U.S. National Archives.

67. Benes, *op. cit.*, p. 197. The meeting was held at Kirsanov, about 100 miles east of Tambov.

68. F.O. 371, vol. 3323.

69. *Ibid.*, Lockhart's cable of May 18, 1918.

purpose of "opposing German aggression and intrigue at Archangel and Murmansk and along the railways leading to those parts", were equally unconvincing — since there was no evidence in those parts of such "aggression and intrigue" from the side of the Germans, who were hundreds of miles away, whereas the Soviet Government had already denounced the Allied landings at Vladivostok as aggression, and their aid to Semyonov as intrigue, in just those terms.

Balfour himself made the purpose of all this shadow-boxing perfectly clear in an irritated comment a few days later, when the C.I.G.S. said that he concurred in the proposed move of the Czechoslovaks to Archangel, but wanted to know what numbers would arrive, what transport was needed, and whether guns and horses were to be embarked or only personnel. The Foreign Secretary minuted: "This seems quite inconsistent with the decision already arrived at that the Czechs should guard the approaches both to Murmansk and Archangel. *There was no question about embarkation*" (*my italics*).[70]

Thereafter although the continuing querulous argument between British and French can be traced in the Foreign Office files, in fact both sides understood that the Czechs were not going to be evacuated, either through the Far East or through the North, but would be staying in Russia as an instrument of anti-Soviet intervention. A cable to Hodgson, the British Consul at Vladivostok, admitted this before long: "In view of the difficulties of trnsportation, it has been decided not to ship the Czech Corps to France at present", with an additional: "Confidential. It might be used in Siberia in connection with Allied intervention, should this materialise".[71]

In this way, *formally* nearly a fortnight before the Czech Legion's insurrection began at Chelyabinsk, on the Trans-Siberian Railway, but *in reality* more than six weeks beforehand, the die had already been cast. The suggestion about using the Czech Legion against the Bolsheviks made by the Allied military representatives at the end of November, 1917, the action desired by Masaryk at that time, and the formal proposal made by the British War Office on March 30, had been put into effect. In the light of all the foregoing, it is obvious that the incidents on the railway (May 28) which have usually been represented as the cause of the Legion's armed attack on the Soviets throughout Eastern Russia were only a pretext, not a real cause — and if that particular pretext had not arisen, another would certainly have been found by the time the Legion had arrived in the Far East, where the Japanese were in occupation with general Allied support, and Ataman Semyonov was carrying on his own war.

70. *Ibid,* Director of Military Intelligence to Gen. Spiers, April 25, 1918.

71. *Ibid.*, Foreign Office to Hodgson, May 16, 1918.

In its own way, and therefore with its own special difficulties of achievement, the involvement of the Czech Legion in war against the Soviet Government was just as much the fulfilment of the Anglo-French master-plan of December 21, 1917, as all the other operations. As Benes himself said in June 1923, during a discussion among the former Legionaries about Czechoslovak-Soviet relations: "For me the most important thing was that our army in Russia, as I understood it, was for the Allies simply a pawn on the chess-board, though a very weighty one: with iron inexorability it was calculated that there were on the spot a certain number of our people, and when it became necessary they would be simply sacrificed... We ourselves could not decide whether to carry out intervention or not to carry it out".[72] The diplomatic papers and letters quoted earlier demonstrate this completely.

Only by ignoring them, and by vainly searching for "documentary evidence" that such-and-such Allied representatives gave such-and-such persons precise instructions in so many terms to revolt, can one continue to sustain the hoary old thesis that there was no "deliberate conspiracy", that "neither side was to blame", that the insurrection of May 28 was due to "the general climate of confusion and suspicion", and so forth.[73]

9

One more form in which the aims of the Balfour Memorandum were pursued deserves its place in the general picture, and should be better known than it has been so far.

Throughout the months after the Memorandum, a British intelligence officer, Captain George A. Hill, was preparing systematically for disruption of the Soviet régime from within. Of necessity his preparations had to be at least as protracted as those of the Czechoslovak leaders, and naturally even more secret. But their character, and their connection with other applications of the general

72. Benes, *Our Revolution* (in Czech, Prague 1923), p. 218.

73. Kennan *op. cit.*, pp. 164-165. M. Pierre Pascal, a lieutenant in the French Military Mission in Russia at the time, has described in his memoirs the hatred of the leaders of the Czechoslovak forces on the Trans-Siberian railway for the Soviets, their first atrocities against the latter, and their retort — when he objected — that they had instructions from the French Ambassador Noulens. *(Mon Journal de Russie, 1916-1918,* Lausanne 1975, pp. 284-293).

plan adopted by the British and French Governments at the end of 1917, are unmistakeable. They stand out very clearly from Captain Hill's report to the Director of Military Intelligence, War Office, dated November 26, 1918, on "work done for the D.M.I. from February 24 until October 2, 1918". Some years later, Capt. Hill published two books on this activity, naturally with many omissions and with compensating literary flourishes, but following parts of his original report pretty closely. In combination with the text of the latter now made available in the Foreign Office files, the two sources leave little room for speculation.[74]

The following picture emerges.

Capt. Hill became an intelligence officer soon after the beginning of the 1914-1918 war. In July, 1917, he was ordered by the Director of Military Intelligence to join a Royal Flying Corps mission in Russia. He worked until the end of September under a member of the staff of Major-General Poole, head of a British Mission first in Petrograd and then at the Russian Army Headquarters. The duties for which he had been sent to Russia "vanished with Kerensky's governement"; and he was then (December, 1917) lent to a Canadian engineer, Col. Boyle, supposedly to help the Soviet authorities in rebuilding Russia's railways, and in particular (he says) cleaning up a big tangle and blockage in the Moscow railway junction. Earlier, in Petrograd, Hill had been asked by the Roumanian Minister to help if possible in transferring Roumanian Crown treasure from Moscow to Jassy: and having secured Soviet permission for this operation, Hill and Boyle reached Jassy on December 24. They handed over the treasure and then (according to Hill's story) assisted materially in securing the signature of a Soviet-Roumanian peace protocol (March 5, 1918).

But before this, as he writes, Capt. Hill had begun operations against the Soviet Government. "Before going to Roumania I had started a little private bureau of information", he wrote in his first book (p. 156). The nature of the bureau was not stated there. But a clue is provided by the entry in his report to the D.M.I. that he "worked with Russian and Roumanian officers stopping sabotage by Bolsheviks in the 4th Army, at the request of General Shcherbachev" (commanding that Army). What "stopping sabotage" meant was that the Roumanian military authorities, on the General's instructions, began disarming revolutionary Russian regiments on their front, breaking up regimental committees, shooting their most active members and seizing regimental food stores. Earlier (December 16, 1917) Shcherbachev had taken advantage of his appointment by the phantom bourgeois Ukrainian government, the

74. F.O. 371, vol. 3350, pp. 16-45 (with maps): and G.A. Hill, D.S.O., *Go Spy The Land* (London, 1932) and *Dreaded Hour* (London, 1936).

"Central Rada", to order the restoration to their posts of all the Tsarist officers whom their soldiers had dismissed in the first weeks after the November revolution.[75] This activity in its turn lends a special colour to the "destruction and sabotage of certain mines" in the Donetz coalfield, which (Capt. Hill reported) he had arranged with a representative of the "miners' union" (in reality, the mine-owners) there during February 1918, i.e. *before* the Germans began occupying the Ukraine.

In mid-March he attended the 4th Congress of Soviets which ratified the Brest-Litovsk Peace Treaty and — with the help of Mr. Wardrop, the British Consul-General in Moscow — met Lieutenant "Reid" (Reilly) of Military Intelligence Section I.c., who was already actively engaged in sabotage. Hill agreed to cooperate with him "where possible". However, he continued openly to wear the uniform of a British officer, now appointed by Trotsky, in his own words, to the post of "Inspector of Aviation". By May, according to his report, Russian flying officers were "getting restless", and he had done "much work among them": the nature of this work is indicated by his note towards the end of April — "propaganda started". By July, under the heading of "Aviation", he reported not only sabotage but "judicious evacuation". What this meant he explained further in his report. Many units of the air force were being sent to the Czecho-slovak front. "As most of the unit commanders were of our orientation, and in league with myself, this was very much encouraged, as we hoped to get whole squadrons deserting to the Tcheko-Slovaks". If a whole squadron deserted, he guaranteed 10,000 roubles to each pilot and 2,500 roubles to each observer. In June, just after the insurrection of the Czechoslovak Legion, he "got into touch with them": and in July he linked up his work of "identification with destruction and recruiting".

This work of "identifications" had begun in the last days of March, 1918, had developed further in April, and had been combined (Hill reported) with similar work by M.I. I.c., i.e. by Reilly. *In his book* Capt. Hill wrote that he had started this work, with Soviet approval, for the purpose of identifying German units present at, or being moved from, the Eastern front, and claimed that "within a few weeks we had a complete net of agents working in all the eastern territories occupied by the Austro-German armies". But *his secret report* gives quite a different picture: "the idea was of course to combine identifications with destruction and recruiting" — and in fact even in his book he more than once paid tribute to the "patriotic" Russian officers... "a splendid band of irregular troops composed of Russian ex-officers" who carried on this work against the Soviet authorities.

75. Mintz, *op. cit.,* vol. III, pp. 580-633.

A courier service, which he started in July, depended almost exclusively on Russian ex-officers, as did his recruiting.

These activities, however, were not only intended to serve the needs of his "private bureau of information", his courier service or his "identifications": nor were they confined to helping the "Tcheko-Slovaks". His reference to the "south" has already been mentioned. Like the other sides of his activity, recruiting for this purpose began to develop rapidly in the summer. His report runs: "Early in July it had become evident that recruits would be wanted very shortly for the North, and therefore a new sub-section to deal with this work was formed. A number of officers of all services were selected and given advances to reach the North. It was realised that all recruiting would have to be on a very limited scale until we had established a front, but it seemed that, once that were done, a large number of recruits could be despatched". Thus the future Archangel front, as well as those on the Don and the Trans-Siberian Railway, were all being provided with officer recruits for the Whites by Capt. Hill, so far as he was able.

Other activities which he listed, during the period before the Allied landing at Archangel brought greatly increased possibilities, were the following:

> "*Station control in Moscow.* As much movement of troops was expected in the Moscow knot (junction) it was decided, in addition to the information got from various sources, to put special agents on all the stations for control.
>
> "*Destruction gangs.* A small destruction gang was organised in July.
>
> "*Passes.* A small section for obtaining false passports, passes and documents was started in July".

As early as March, 1918 (Capt. Hill made clear in his first book) he was "constantly in touch" with the secret counter-revolutionary organisation set up by Boris Savinkov, which included not only members of his own Socialist-Revolutionary party, but also officers of the former Imperial Army. "I was kept informed" of all Savinkov's plans for a rising at Yaroslavl, Hill added.[76] The rising took place on July 6, 1918, and was only suppressed a fortnight later, with extensive bloodshed and destruction of property on both sides.

Reading both his secret report and Capt. Hill's first book, one is struck by the relatively large resources of which he disposed for his work. Indeed he wrote of his secret organisation in his first book (p. 197): "This required arms, money, passes and most of all direction, with all of which I supplied them". Only one passage in his second book threw some partial light on the origin of his funds. He wrote: "I

---

76. *Go Spy The Land,* pp. 196, 202.

had arranged to finance my work through sources within the country".[77] Most probably this finance was supplied from the rouble funds still possessed by the former owners and officials of the nationalised banks and commercial concerns, in exchange for sterling or drafts on British banks. It was by this means (as the Foreign Office records show) that Lockhart was able from April onwards to supply large sums to various other counter-revolutionary organisations (a million roubles to the "National Centre" in July, 10 millions to Alexeyev on the Don, jointly with the French, and so forth).[78]

Throughout these months Capt. Hill conducted his activities — which included not only gathering information, the normal purpose of intelligence work, but also promoting sabotage, wrecking of public property, and aid to military conspiracies and insurrections against the Soviet Government — while formally an accepted officer of a foreign and nominally friendly army, but actually leading, as he wrote himself, "a double life". Part of the time, he said, he was in the uniform of a British officer, and the rest of the time in mufti, visiting his agents in different parts of Moscow on foot.[79]

Quite naturally, Hill was kept fully aware of Lieut. Reilly's now well-known plans for persuading — or more accurately bribing — the Lettish Rifle Regiment in Moscow to revolt against the Soviet Government. Like Mr. Lockhart, he gave no hint of any active part played by himself in these plans, presenting matters as though he was a mere passive spectator. But it is not without interest that after the conspiracy had failed, when Mr. Lockhart had been arrested while he himself was obliged to go underground, he was moved to select a few sympathisers among the Letts to go secretly into Latvia. His report to the War Office ran: "As we have already spent so much money, it was worth spending some more to save something of the wreck. I therefore collected half a dozen Letts personally known to me, and sent them off on an anti-Bolshevik campaign... to work in Riga, Mitau and Pernau". These towns were now in German occupation, but it was against the powerful Bolshevik underground that Capt. Hill sent them to work, not against the Germans.[80]

Thus, while supposedly cooperating with the Soviet authorities and ostensibly concerned with action against Germany, Capt. Hill too was playing his part, "as quietly as possible" for war on the Bolsheviks. It would be wrong, however, to suppose that his activities — and those of others — were entirely unknown to at any rate one section of the Soviet authorities. A message to the Foreign Office

77. G.A. Hill, *Dreaded Hour,* p.11.

78. Ullman, *op. cit.,* pp. 231, 232, 292.

79. *Go Spy The Land,* p. 202.

80. F.O. 371, vol. 3350, p. 43.

from Lockhart as early as February 2, 1918, is very enlightening in this respect. "I cannot help feeling that even at the present moment the Bolshevik Government dislikes the idea of a rupture with England. This is proved by its reluctance to expose our intrigues in this country, which are well known to them and which certainly exceed anything that Russian agents have done or are doing in England".[81]

Apart from Capt. Hill's work and from the Reilly conspiracy, however, one other clandestine British organisation operating from early on against the Soviet régime, and preparing to do more, should at least be mentioned. This was conducted by Captain Cromie, R.N., who had been left in the British Embassy at Petrograd in the position of acting Naval Attaché when the Ambassador and the rest of his staff had left in February. It will be sufficient (in addition to the general allusions made by Mr. Lockhart in his "Memoirs of a British Agent") to quote some relevant disclosures made by the opening of the Foreign Office archives.

One is a cable from Mr. F.O. Lindley, at Petrograd, transmitting a message from Capt. Cromie to the Director of Naval Intelligence on February 22, 1918. "All signs of effective control have disappeared in the Baltic Fleet. I have every hope of organising the destruction of valuable ships with the aid of Admiral Rogvorov and Admiral Bacherev". A second is a cable from Lockhart on May 25: "If we are to intervene without Bolshevik agreement, as now seems probable, it will be absolutely necessary for us to destroy the Baltic Fleet. I have had several conversations with Capt. Cromie on this subject. As you are aware, he has made arrangements of his own towards this object. The destruction of the Fleet should take place almost simultaneously with our intervention" (initialled at the Foreign Office by Lord Curzon, Lord Hardinge and Mr. Balfour). A third is a message sent from Stockholm by the British Minister on September 7, 1918, saying that a secretary of the American Embassy in Russia, Norman Armour, had told him when passing through that "in Moscow three weeks ago Lockhart had told him he had had the opportunity to buy off Lettish troops, that the scheme was known to and approved by the French and American Consuls, but that he, Armour, had no knowledge of the supposed coup d'état for September 10, reported by the Bolsheviks to have been discovered, and did not believe it was true. He presumed the Letts' Commander had given the show away. As regards Petrograd, he had seen Cromie two days before the attack on the Embassy. He thought the secret documents the Bolsheviks claimed to have taken were Cromie's lists of Russians to be recruited, etc. He was not aware that Cromie had anything to do with Lockhart's schemes in Moscow regarding the Lettish regiments". A fourth is the

81. F.O. 371, vol. 3298.

statement drafted in the Foreign Office on September 9, on the news of Cromie's being shot dead after he had shot two of the Red Guards raiding the Embassy building. Referring to Cromie's preparations for destroying the Baltic Fleet, it continued: "These activities, carried on for months in daily danger of his life, brought him inevitably into cooperation with Russians hostile to the Bolshevik régime. His plans may very well have included the destruction of certain bridges as the Bolsheviks declare".[82]

Thus Capt. Cromie's activities, too, while conducted "as quietly as possible", fitted precisely into the general plan laid down by Mr. Balfour and endorsed by the War Cabinet on December 21, 1917, as a guide to action by the various Departments of State represented in it or controlled by it.

---

82. F.O. 371, vol. 3315, cable received February 24, 1918; F.O. 371, vol. 3286, cable received May 29, 1918; F.O. 371, vol. 3336, cable received September 8, 1918; F.O. 175, Box 1.

PART III

10

Among all these secret preparations for attacking the Soviet Republic, all round its borders and from within, it would have been surprising had none been made in connection with Archangel, which had such a long history as a port of entry into Russia, primarily for British trade. But the preliminary difficulties here were even greater than were involved in the revolt of the Czechoslovak Legion. The possibility of preparatory intrigue among elements of the local population was pitifully small. There was no anti-Soviet movement in the neighbouring regions for hundreds of miles east, south or west. The pretext of combatting German influence, even a German military threat, was too ludicrous to deceive anyone — except a public nearly two thousand miles away, ignorant of geography and deluged with wartime propaganda. There was not even the preliminary foothold on Russian soil which the Allies had had at Murmansk since 1916, which they began to expand by additional landings in March, 1918. Nothing but direct and open invasion was practically possible in the case of Archangel. And evidently for this very reason the discussion of the question, "as far as possible", took place without the knowledge of the British Consul in the city: indeed, his daily activities and contacts with the local Soviet were, for the Foreign Office, the War Office, the Admiralty and other departments involved, a convenient screen for the preliminaries of invasion.

It is not out of place here to record an optimistic picture of what victory over the Bolsheviks would have meant for Archangel which was drawn by one who later became a main organiser of invasion there. This was Major-General Poole, who as we have seen knew Russian conditions to some extent from his work with the Tsarist Army, and actually had had experience at Archangel at that time. Before leaving Moscow at the end of February, 1918, in a letter to the Enemy Supplies Restriction Department in London, he wrote that the country was "slowly but very surely toppling over", and that before long there would be "a mighty crash". Therefore it was urgent to make preparation to get hold of trade with Russia after the war. "Of all the schemes I have heard, the one I like best is to boost up the Northern Federation with Archangel as its centre" (it will be recalled that Young had reported a scheme to create such a "Federation"). Poole continued, anticipating the optimism of later months: "There we could easily consolidate the Government — one Man-of-War in the harbour would do that. We could reap a rich harvest in timber and railway concessions and control the two Northern Ports".[83]

However, several months of discussion had to go by before action could be taken to bring this attractive prospect nearer. In the meantime the Foreign Office began to listen cautiously to advice like the following.

On May 11, 1918, Mr. Lindley (Counsellor of the British Embassy) commented that a French proposal to send a Chargé d'Affaires to Russia seemed out of place if there were to be armed intervention at Port Arthur, as he understood was the intention. "I trust the importance of sending some force to Archangel to safeguard the stores will not be lost sight of". Thus plans for intervention from the sea at both ends of Russia seemed, in his mind at least, to be closely linked.[84]

Three days later the Foreign Office received a strongly worded letter from the Capt. Alex Proctor already mentioned, signing himself as representing: "The British Military Mission of Supply to Russia, The Army Contract Department and the Restriction of Enemy Supplies Department". He advocated "the immediate armed occupation of Archangel" as "the only means whereby the least semblance of Allied influence can be retained in European Russia". It would lead to the immediate "reinforcement of loyal patriotic Russians". Moreover his views were strongly endorsed, he said, by "Mr. Ernest Wilson, Chief of Malcolm and Co., the largest Flax and Hemp Exporting House in Russia, and during the war head of the War Office Flax Purchasing Committee in Russia, with twenty years' experience in Russia" (Mr. Proctor's capitals).[85] In this letter he described Lockhart — who at that time was still opposing armed intervention — as a "simpleton". In a talk at the Foreign Office a few days later, again pressing for intervention, Proctor this time denounced Lockhart as "either a fool or a traitor" and he would hang him.[86] This was because Lockhart was proposing some sort of cooperation with the Soviet Government to rebuild its armed forces — of course in the hope that they would be involved in fighting with the Germans.

Obviously Capt. Proctor was not the only purveyor of such views

83. F.O. 371, vol. 3318, letter of January 19, 1918.

84. F.O. 371, vol. 3299, cable via Stockholm.

85. F.O. 371, vol. 3290, letter of March 14, 1918.

86. F.O. 371, vol. 3305, recorded conversation of March 19, 1918.

about Archangel. There is a relevant minute of discussions 48 hours later at the Inter-Departmental Committee mentioned previously: "It was agreed at the Russia Committee that more harm than good would be done by sounding Trotsky" (then People's Commissar for War) "on the Archangel question".[87] And indeed we find almost immediately a note by the Marquess Curzon of Kedleston himself: "The majority of our advisers tell us that to help to create a new State or a new Army in Russia out of the shattered débris of Bolshevism is a fantastic dream. Meanwhile we have Gen. Poole advising the occupation of Murmansk and Archangel".[88]

Moreover, Admiral Kemp at Murmansk had already at the beginning of the month been pressing for the military occupation of that town: and although the Army Council decided not to send troops there, the Admiral adopted the simple device of landing 120 British Marines — a move which, an American representative in London told the Foreign Office, had "aroused surprise".[89]

Kemp now asked for authority to issue a declaration that the British Government had no intention of *occupying* the Murman region — a request which produced illuminating comments at the Foreign Office. "It is impossible to give a full declaration without tying our hands" (E.H. Carr); "It has been found practically impossible to frame a declaration... We should pursue the same course in regard to Archangel and make no declaration at all" (Sir R. Graham). Thereupon Kemp asked for authority to state officially that Great Britain had "no intention of *annexing part* of the Murmansk district", while continuing to assist it to maintain its independence (of Moscow). This authority was given, whereupon he reported that he had made the declaration asked for to the Murmansk District Soviet, and it had been "well received".[90] It will be recalled that the same ambiguous declaration was made at Archangel a few days later.

Meanwhile, however, the War Cabinet had already approved a message to Lord Reading (British Ambassador at Washington) referring to the "great danger of the Germans gaining the upper hand in Russia", and to the need for "the presence of Allied forces at such ports as Murmansk, Archangel and Vladivostok".[91] By this time of course the Japanese invasion at Vladivostok was already ten days old: a fact which evidently decided M. Lockhart in Moscow to change

---

87. F.O. 371, vol. 3283, Minute of March 21, 1918.

88. *Ibid.,* memorandum of March 26, 1918.

89. F.O. 371, vol. 3307, papers dated March 2, 26 and 29, 1918.

90. *Ibid.*, Kemp's cable of March 31, Foreign Office comments of April 12 and Kemp's further cables of April 15 and 25.

91. *Ibid.,* minute of April, 15, 1918.

his previous attitude of opposition to intervention. On May 4 he cabled that "intervention at Murmansk, Archangel and in the Far East must be prepared at once with all possible activity. Archangel is an essential point if we are to obtain any support whatever from Russian sources" (i.e. from the anti-Bolsheviks). Foreign Office comments on this were conditioned as yet by the impossibility of providing large forces for intervention (this was the period of the temporary interlude between the two phases — March and May — of the big German offensive on the Western Front). "I much doubt whether military operations on any large scale at Murmansk and Archangel are feasible" wrote Curzon; and: "The military authorities have throughout declared the impossibility of providing troops for Murmansk and Archangel", wrote Lord Hardinge, the Permanent Under-Secretary.[92]

Accordingly their first move was to press Lockhart to secure from the Soviet Government "a definite invitation to intervene for the protection of Russia and Russian interests". But his reply was to press for intervention without Soviet consent, because "it is now clear to everyone, and to no one more clear than to the Bolsheviks themselves, that in accepting intervention they sign their own death warrant".[93] This indeed was only too obvious from what was going on already in the Far East and on the Don.

Accordingly, a decisive step was taken by the War Cabinet, on a minute submitted by the Foreign Office on May 11, 1918. The decision ran:

"1. Gen. Poole to go as soon as possible to Russia to advise the War Office as to all steps to be taken in regard to our intervention in Russia.
2. Officers and N.C.O.s to be collected to assist him in the task of organising Czecho-Slovak and other forces of intervention at Archangel and Murmansk.
3. First Sea Lord undertook to send 200 marines for the defence of Archangel, and the War Office to send such munitions and supplies as Gen. Poole might deem necessary for the purpose of his mission.
4. Gen. Poole was to consider, while holding and safeguarding the positions at Murmansk and Archangel, how far he could work up from Archangel towards Vologda with the forces at his disposal.
5. Undue weight had been placed in our recent correspon-

92. *Ibid.*, Cable received from Lockhart on May 6, 1918.

93. *Ibid.*, Foreign Office cable of May 8, 1918 and Lockhart's reply of May 9, received May 13, 1918.

dence on the desirability of an invitation for intervention from the Bolshevik Government".[94]

The references to the Czechoslovaks and to "working up towards Vologda" were, of course, a reflection of prevalent delusions about the feebleness of Soviet resistance: but so far as intervention at Archangel was concerned, this was the turn to action. It was not surprising that President Wilson, when in conversation with the British Ambassador on May 22, while still thinking the moment as yet "inopportune" for intervention in Siberia, "drew a distinction between intervention in Siberia and intervention to protect Murmansk and Archangel". Lord Reading "did not pursue this subject".[95]

In fact, the Admiralty had already sent a message to Kemp at Murmansk, on a reported German threat to the Soviet Government about the Allied forces in that port, that their withdrawal from the Murmansk coast "would make our proposed action at Archangel impossible, and the Allies have no intention of evacuating North Russia".[96]

Finally, on May 23, "the War Cabinet ordered the despatch to North Russia of a military training mission and a small expeditionary force. The expeditionary force... was to aid in defending the Murmansk region against expected attacks from White Finns and Germans. The training mission, comprising some 560 officers and other ranks drawn from all arms and services, was to accompany the expeditionary force and proceed as soon as the ice melted to Archangel, in order to train and equip the Czech troops supposedly on their way there, and also local Russians who, it was anticipated, would volunteer. Both British contingents were to be under the command of Major-General F.C. Poole".[97]

Thereafter the preparations for intervention at Archangel — including the decision of the Allied Supreme War Council at Versailles on June 3, in effect endorsing the British War Cabinet's decision (enlarged by the provision of "four to six British, French, American or Italian battalions to be sent to occupy Murmansk and Archangel"[98] — were a matter of detail. The propagandists of intervention like Lockhart and Wardrop in Moscow, Cromie and Wood-

94. *Ibid.*, G.T. 4519. War Cabinet decision, "Intervention in Russia", May 20, 1918. Kennan *op. cit.* pp. 263-41 gives a summary.

95. *Ibid.*, Cable from Washington, received May 24, 1918.

96. F.O. 371, vol. 3307, cable of May 18, 1918.

97. British General Staff "Diary of Events in Russia and Siberia, December, 1917 to December, 1918", quoted by Ullman, *op. cit.*, pp. 172-173.

98. F.O. 371, vol. 3286, Treasury memorandum of June 8, 1918, summarising decisions of the Supreme War Council.

house in Petrograd, were pressing for the largest possible forces to be sent, while the London authorities realised that the very large expedition which was being suggested ("at least two divisions", said Lockhart on June 21) was quite out of the question. It is not necessary here to examine the details.

What is important is that by the beginning of June, 1918, the general directive of the War Cabinet on December 21, 1917, was at last in active application at Archangel too. The landing by British, French and American forces, postponed once or twice but finally begun on August 2, was predetermined. This was not only in spite of the very full and thoughtful protest against any such scheme sent to his chiefs by Felix Cole, U.S. Vice-Consul at Archangel on June 1. It was also in spite of the increasing protests by Douglas Young, Cole's colleague and friend.[99]

Appendix to Chapter 10

In Moscow at this time there was a French military mission, headed by Colonel (later General) Lavergne. One of his staff, concerned with Allied propaganda in Russia, was a twenty-five-year old graduate, Lieut. Pierre Pascal. He was making daily notes of facts which came to his notice, including important telegrams which he had to cypher and decypher. The French Ambassador Noulens was at the dates mentioned below away in Finland, but the mission was in constant touch with him. Here are three entries in Pascal's diary, following the ratification of the German-Soviet peace treaty of Brest-Litovsk:

> "20 March 1918. A mad scheme of the Ambassador: occupation of Archangel, Murmansk, Vologda, make use of the Czechs and instal a new Government.
>
> "21 March 1918. At 4 pm, a telegram (from France) in reply to the great scheme of the Ambassador on measures for inter-Allied

99. Cole's message is summarised by Kennan, *op.cit.,* pp. 363-364. Cole said that north Russia "was no-where near as pro-Ally as it might be.": "that intervention could not reckon on active support from Russians": that the political groups advocating intervention — Socialist-Revolutionaries, Mensheviks and Cadets — were "discredited office-holders seeking to regain power": that Russian opinion would be "directed not by them but by the Bolshevik leaders": that intervention would "alienate thousands of anti-German Bolsheviks": and that intervention would "belie all our promises to the Russian people made since October 26, 1917".

> occupation of Archangel and Murmansk and for landing a division. He is advised not to ask for the agreement of the Soviet Government, but to act on his own."

Later, Paris agreed to second forty French officers to help in building up the new Red Army. But then:

> "7 April 1918. A telegram from Paris says: don't support the formation of a Russian army: it would be a menace to the social order in general, and might offer resistance to action by the Japanese."

Pascal wrote down: "And so it is true: out of hatred for Socialism we have sold Russia to Japan. These days I am truly ashamed to be a Frenchman."*

11

Young was not informed either of the War Cabinet's attitude expressed in the cable to Washington on April 15, or of its decision of May 11, nor yet of the Allied Supreme War Council's decision of June 3. But as was shown earlier, he had twice in April warned the Foreign Office that the Archangel Soviet was fully alive to the danger of forcible action by the Allies at that port. So acute was the tension that on April 29 he had asked for an assurance that neither aggression nor occupation was intended: in reply, the Foreign Office had authorised him on May 4 to make the same ambiguous declaration that had been made by Admiral Kemp at Murmansk. This was published in the press over Young's signature, and had somewhat allayed suspicions for a time.

Nevertheless, the same reports that had alerted Cole were available to Young; in addition, Lockhart's messages for General Poole from Moscow were being routed through Archangel, and showed that Lockhart now was also pressing for invasion. In May, as Young recorded later, he had to supply five Americans who had been engaged in preparing the notorious "Sisson documents" (forgeries purporting to show that the Bolsheviks were German agents) with false papers as "British seamen", to enable them to get away from Archangel on a British ship. This increased his disquiet; and messages from General Poole, following his arrival at Murmansk, did

---

* P. Pascal, *Mon Journal de Russie, 1916-1918*. Lausanne, 1975, pp. 265, 270.

nothing to allay it. Finally, when the French Consul, after visiting the French Ambassador at Vologda, returned to Archangel (Young wrote in his unpublished memoir), "the present writer asked him, with incredulity, whether he thought the Allied Governments were going to be mad enough to intervene by force. The French Consul replied, with a cynical smile of evident satisfaction: 'I don't think it; I know it' ".

Accordingly, on June 6, 1918, Young sent the following cable to the Foreign Office:

> "*Urgent.* Rumours of active Allied intervention at Archangel in the near future are current here, and such a policy seems to be in high favour with the newly-arrived French Consul and Military Mission."

In view of the formal assurances given by Allied representatives at Murmansk and repeated here by him with Foreign Office sanction he had hitherto discredited these rumours.

> "I have now however received from General Poole at Murmansk a request to find accommodation at Archangel for 600 officers and other British ratings, and the impression that active measures are contemplated is otherwise confirmed.
>
> "Being completely in the dark as to the nature and extent of the operations contemplated, and of the advantages which His Majesty's Government hope to derive from them," Young said he could not express a fair opinion even as to their probable local effect. "In the absence of such data, I would however like to record my conviction that any premature military operations carried out without the consent of the de facto local authorities will be attended with grave risks: and without bringing any great permanent advantage will, even if successful locally, commit His Majesty's Government to ever-increasing obligations from which they will be unable to free themselves without discredit and loss of prestige".

The most he had ever suggested was that Allied cruisers should be present as a passive force in the first instance, "in order to give local influences favourable to us an opportunity of declaring themselves".

Thus Young as yet was by no means excluding the possibility of military operations altogether, provided they were not "premature": or of the local authorities consenting to such operations, as had happened at Murmansk: or of the presence of British warships encouraging pro-Ally i.e. anti-Bolshevik elements to "declare themselves". He was still under the influence of the anti-Bolshevik feelings which he, and others like him, had experienced in consequence of the October Revolution.

The Foreign Office comment (signed "G.N.C.", i.e. Lord Curzon) was that Young seemed "to have read an extended meaning" into previous communications with him; and the reply sent to him on June 12 read: "There is no intention to undertake premature military operations, but it is essential for the Allies to keep Murmansk and Archangel open, and to take precautions to secure this end. The large number of officers referred to are sent to take charge of Czech detachments. Guarantees given in my telegram of non-intervention in Russian affairs and of absence of annexationist aims of course still hold good".[100]

Young of course could not know that by now there was no question of the Czechs coming to Archangel. But he was aware that the Allies were fully involved in massive operations on the Western Front. And in any case the assurances given by Curzon were obviously double-edged, and could not persuade Young. On June 19 he therefore sent a further warning:

> "I have trustworthy secret information that the local representatives of the Central Authority have received instructions from Lenin to make immediate preparations with a view to the destruction of explosives and ammunition stored at Archangel. This would probably result in great damage to the town and blocking the river below Archangel. Mining of the channel is also to be feared.
>
> "It is not known whether these measures are aimed against a westward advance of the Czechs or suspected Allied occupation, but probably both: and if the scheme were carried out as Allied ships enter, the disastrous results are obvious.
>
> "The plan is apparently being worked over the heads and without the knowledge of the local authorities, who would scarcely sanction proceedings so detrimental to local interests. If therefore execution of this scheme seems imminent, pending your (reply or) General Poole's arrival, I propose to appeal to the local authorities to take action to prevent it, if necessary using the foodstuffs on the store-ships as an argument.
>
> "It is impossible to say whether the intentions are really serious, but in any case an uninterrupted entry into Archangel should not be taken for granted".[101]

The essential point, of course, was in the last paragraph — and in any case no reply had been received by Young before he sent another cable on June 22, demanding to be "informed fully of the policy or policies being followed by His Majesty's Government regarding Archangel and Russia generally". He went on:

---

100. This exchange of messages is in F.O., 371, vol. 3286, pp. 161-162 and 164.

101. F.O. 371, vol. 3305, p. 489.

1. *Douglas Young in 1909; his first vice-consular appointment in Zanzibar.*

2. *Douglas Young in 1919.*

3. *Archangel port and roadstead, 1917.*

4. *Archangel from the river Northern Dvina, 1917.*

5. *Celebrating the March Revolution in 1917.*

6. *British bluejackets landing, 1918.*

7. *A British tank, 1919 (still on show in Archangel).*

8. *The "Dyer Battalion" (Slavo-British Legion) on parade, 1919.*

9. *"The powers that be are tearing their hair." Bank notes printed in London for the Whites.*

МАНДАТ.

№ 5093

Пред'явитель сего тов. Пластинина Ревекка Акибовна есть член Архангельского Губернского Исполнительного Комитета Советов Рабочих, Крестьянских и Красноармейских Депутатов, выбранный на «4» Губернском С'езде Советов Секретарем-членом Президиума Губисполкома

Заведывающий Архангельским Губернским Отделом Управления

«7» Августа 1920 г.

Гор. Архангельск

Секретарь

10. *The membership credential of Revekka Plastinina, secretary to the Presidium of the Archangel Soviet.*

11. *Pavlin Vinogradov, vice-chairman of the Archangel Soviet, and first organiser of armed resistance to the Allied invasion.*

РОССІЙСКАЯ КОММУНИСТИЧЕСКАЯ ПАРТІЯ (БОЛЬШЕВИКОВ).

Пролетаріи всѣх стран, соединяйтесь!

АРХАНГЕЛЬСКАЯ ПРАВДА

Органъ Арх. Ком. Рос. Коммун. Партіи (б-ков).

Цѣна отдѣльнаго № **25** коп.

ПОДПИСНАЯ ЦѢНА: на 1 мѣс.—3 руб. на 3 мѣс.—8 руб. на 6 мѣс.—17 руб.

Адрес Редакціи и Конторы:
г. Архангельск, «Клуб Коммунистов».
Телефоны: № 3—72 и 5-44.
Контора открыта с 10 ч. у. до 4 ч. дня ежедневно, кромѣ праздников.
Пріем по дѣлам редакціи ежедн. с 5 до 9 ч. в.

№ 5. — Выходит 3 раза в недѣлю. — 17 Іюля 1918 г.

В Кеми английскими генералами разогнан уѣздный Совѣт и разстрѣляны члены президіума Совѣта т. т. Масорин и Каменев и секретарь т. Ежов. Населеніе силой принуждается вступать в англійскую армію.

Рабочіе и крестьяне! Вот какія дѣла слѣдуют за „сладкими“ словами англо-французских разбойников о „невмѣшательствѣ“ в наши дѣла.

ЗНАЙТЕ-ЖЕ, ЧТО АНГЛО-ФРАНЦУЗСКІЕ ГЕНЕРАЛЫ НЕ ЧИЩЕ ГЕРМАНСКИХ, И В СЛУЧАѢ УСПѢХА АНГЛО-ФРАНЦУЗСКОЙ ЗАТѢИ НА СѢВЕРѢ, НАС ЖДЕТ ТО-ЖЕ, ЧТО ПОСТИГЛО НАШИХ БРАТЬЕВ НА УКРАИНѢ.

Рабочіе и крестьяне! К оружію! Всѣ в ряды Красной Рабоче-Крестьянской Арміи!

Извѣщенія и постановленія Центральных Совѣтских учрежденій, Губ. Исп. Ком., Гор. Исп. Ком., Арханг. и Центр. Ком. Рос. Комм. Партіи (б-ков).

От врачебно-санитарнаго отдѣла Губисполкома обращеніе к населенію города Архангельска.

В виду наличности холеры в Петроградѣ и в Поволжьѣ и опасности быстраго занесенія ея в Архангельск, населеніе города Архангельска приглашается на противохолерныя прививки.

Прививки производятся безплатно в слѣдующих пунктах:

1) На Быку—в амбулаторіи союза городов против трамвайнаго парка.

2) В городской амбулаторіи—Петроградскій, 49, около Сѣнной площади.

3) В амбулаторіи Больничнаго городка у баталіона—Вятская улица.

4) В Соломбалѣ—городская амбулаторія по Преображенскому проспекту.

5) В городском пріемном покоѣ порта—угол Набережной и Театральной.

6) Бакарица—в амбулаторіи порта.

7) Экономія—тоже.

8) На пристани бывшей Сѣверна го пароходства—в амбулаторіи.

Прививки начнутся с понедѣльника, 15 іюля, при чем время прививок в первых четырех пунктах опредѣлено от 9 ч. утра до 3 ч. дня.

В Среду, 17 іюля, в 6 час. веч., состоится Общее Собраніе членов Росс. Комм. Партіи (большевиков) гор. Архангельска и всѣх его раіонов. Порядок дня: 1. Текущій момент. 2. Организація военнаго отряда коммунистов. 3. Об «Архангельской Правдѣ». Явка всѣх обязательна. Опозданіе недопустимо.

За Секретаря К-та *А. Попов.*

Слѣдующій № „Архангельской Правды“ выйдет в Четверг, 18 Іюля вечером.

Почему мы призываем дать отпор англо-французским имперіалистам.

Волею II-го Губернскаго Съѣзда Совѣтов рабочих и крестьянских депутатов по Архангельской губерніи объявлена мобилизація рабочих и крестьян.

Для чего? Для того, чтобы создать у нас сильную, могучую Красную Рабоче-Крестьянскую Армію, которая смогла бы дать отпор покушающимся на наш Сѣвер англо-французским имперіалистам.

Наша Совѣтская Республика, гдѣ буржуазія и помѣщики повергнуты, гдѣ у власти рабочій и крестьянин, гдѣ рабоче-крестьянская власть отняла землю у вампиров-помѣщиков и передала ее трудовому народу, гдѣ рабоче-крестьянская власть установила рабочій контроль на фабриках и заводах, положившій конец безпредѣльной эксплуатаціи труда капиталом,—наша Совѣтская Республика представляет собою заразительный примѣр для трудящихся масс всего міра, которыя, глядя на нашу побѣду над *нашими* угнетателями, вступают в борьбу со *своими* угнетателями. Что наша Революція заразила рабочих других стран, что она вызвала в них желаніе, которое с каждым днем усиливается и крѣпнет, помѣряться силами со своими эксплуататорами-капиталистами, видно из тѣх многочисленных сообщеній из Германіи, Австріи, Англіи и Франціи и др. стран, в которых говорится о происходящих там забастовках, об уличных демонстраціях и выступленіях рабочих, о массовых митингах протеста против войны и затѣявших ее правительств и, наконец, о созданіи по подобію наших боевых организацій, Совѣтов рабочих депутатов в цѣлом рядѣ городов Зап. Европы.

И естественно, что капиталисты ненавидят нашу Революцію, ненавидят нашу Совѣтскую Республику, которая своим красным примѣром подымает против них рабочія массы. И понятно, что капиталисты всѣх стран стараются всѣми способами погубить нас, стереть с лица земли Совѣтскую Россію, чтоб убрать с глаз своих рабочих масс этот „опасный примѣр“.

Вот почему капиталисты всѣх стран одинаковые враги наши: как капиталисты Германіи и Австріи, так и капиталисты Англіи и Франціи и Америки.

И если б у нас хватило сил, мы должны были бы всѣм им головы снести.

Но у нас таких сил нѣт. В этом мы должны признаться.

Мы не можем объявить войну капиталистам всего міра. Пока арміи послушны им, они гораздо силь-

12. *"Archangel Pravda", 17 July 1918, reporting the shooting of three members of the Kem Town Soviet by British forces.*

"You have defined the policy as non-annexation and non-interference in internal affairs, and have given guarantees. Yet messages arriving from Lockhart for General Poole make it clear that active intervention has almost passed the stage of discussion. The latter policy cannot bc reconciled with the former, and if carried out in spite of the guarantees will bring your good word into discredit.

"The unaccountable delay of General Poole for several weeks at Murmansk has produced deadlock here, and together with the open secrecy surrounding his coming (e.g. the sending of Russian officers from Moscow to Archangel, apparently to join the British expeditionary force, etc.) wild rumour, suspicions and tension which only needs an incautious even if innocent movement on the part of the Allies to explode. See my immediately preceding telegram regarding the possibility of the war stores being blown up, etc...

"(Groups missing *A.R.*) They" (evidently war-ships *A.R.*) "should be kept away fro the present. At Murmansk they would be within easy call. A (straight forward) statement of policy is most desirable to clear the atmosphere, and Mr. Lindley's speedy arrival without secrecy on a merchant ship should have a good effect. His mission may be too late to attain much practical result, but at least it can do no harm".[102]

On the same day, Young followed up this cable with another urgent communication, saying that the President of the Archangel Regional Executive Committee had requested the removal from the port of Archangel without delay of all British vessels of war. The request added that, "in view of the international and political situation", the arrival of a foreign warship at Archangel would be "regarded as the beginning of active operations which may have the most serious consequences". Young said he had told the President that he had referred the request to London for instructions.[103]

This obviously quite desperate attempt by Young to prevent an armed incursion caused the Foreign Office acute embarrassment. One comment read: "I sympathise with Mr. Young's position, and it is clearly impossible to offer any real opinion on the food question until we decide definitely whether a serious attempt is going to be made to hold Archangel or not. In the meantime we must make some attempt, with the rather inadequate materials at our disposal, to define our policy to Mr. Young". This might be to say that "our present object at Archangel" was to protect Allied stores, and "to prepare the ground for possible intervention of a more active

102. F.O. 371. vol. 3305, pp. 501-502, 504-506.
103. F.O. 371. vol. 3305, p. 497.

character", the prospects of which would depend on "(a) the strength of the forces which we can ourselves spare (b) the number of Russians or non-Russians in Russia who rally to our support (c) the state of opinion in Russia both local and general". The feeling at Archangel seemed to him "somewhat excited", and he thought Mr. Young might find it desirable to issue "a soothing communiqué". This, apart from repeating previous assurances given on May 4, should declare that any Allied action would be directed not against Russia or against any party, "but solely to strengthening Russia and helping to organise her to resist the enemy". Any landing of armed forces would have for its object "(i) to protect Allied stores and prevent Lenin blowing them up, with the probable result of the destruction of the town (ii) to strengthen the hands of the local authorities who appear at present to be prevented by the Central Government from concluding with the Allies a bargain which is manifestly both just and in their own interests".

Such a "soothing communiqué", with its suggestion that armed intervention was intended only to "strengthen Russia" (as, Archangel people might say, had been done in the Far East), to help to "reorganise" her (as the Japanese and the Cossack generals on the Don were doing, by dissolving the Soviets) and to "strengthen" the local Soviets against "Lenin", obviously presented such unenviable prospects that Lord Robert Cecil and Lord Curzon both politely disavowed it. They advised waiting to hear Lindley's views after he had reached Archangel — and asking the Director of Military Intelligence to suggest to General Poole "the desirability of keeping the 1500 troops at Murmansk for the moment". But Lord Hardinge (with the concurrence of Mr. Balfour) said that Mr. Young "seems in an excited state at present, partly because he does not understand the situation, which may be our fault for not having sufficiently explained it to him." Lindley's arrival might "tend to put him straight" — but he might be given "some explanation as suggested above".[104]

These sage comments were dated June 24. Before their tenor could be communicated to Young, a cable from Lindley in Murmansk arrived the next day which evidently acted as a cold douche. He wrote that he agreed with Young "that in view of the local conditions at Archangel and the extremely small force available for occupation of the town i.e. some 300 men, it would be preferable to postpone military occupation until the situation is clearer and until larger forces are available here. If we attempt to land unsuccessfully or are ejected soon after we arrive, we shall lose all our supporters in the country

---

104. F.O. 371, vol. 3305, pp. 497, 501-502, 504-506.

and shall be unable to recover the lost ground later". On the evening of the same day, Lindley reported in a further cable: "At a conference this morning with the First Lord of the Admiralty, it was decided to postpone the military occupation of Archangel until our forces were more adequate and until the position there had been cleared up."

One of the Foreign Office staff minuted: "We ought now to inform Mr. Young of this decision, which may soothe his feelings and relieve the tension for the moment. We can, I fear, give him no indication as to future policy".[105]

While waiting for the position in Archangel to be "cleared up" — which in all probability, from what was said about subsequent events, meant waiting for a promised rising — Young had some very trying moments.

One was in connection with the withdrawal from the port of the British armed ice-breaker *Alexander.* Admiral Kemp reported afterwards that this was done after "an unprovoked hostile demonstration" by Russian ships in the port and field guns ashore.[106] Here is Douglas Young's account, in his unpublished memoir.

> "The present writer played the part of an official inside observer of the 'incident' in question, and the following is his account of what he saw and heard.
>
> "The French Military Mission had diverted to Archangel some Serbian and a few Italian soldiers, with the definite purpose of using them in the proposed anti-Bolshevik 'rising'. The utterance of the Serbian officers in 'White' Russian society, and even their actions in public, were so indiscreet as to make it impossible for the Bolsheviks not to smell a rat. Late at night on July 1 I received reliable information from friendly Russian sources that the Soviet authorities intended on the following morning to disarm the Serbian and Italian troops; and that, as a precaution against the possibility of *Alexander* cooperating with them to resist the disarmament, the ice-breaker was to be masked during the operation by the large Russian ice-breaker *Sviatogor* and some armed trawlers. I arranged for the Commander of *Alexander* to be informed, as it was undesirable that he should come ashore. The next morning I was asked by telephone to go round and see the Executive Committee, and I found my French colleague already there. We were told, quite politely, exactly what I had heard the previous night. The French Consul started to be rude and provocative, informing the members of the Committee that they would

105. F.O. 371, vol. 3319, cables received on April 25 and 27, 1918.
106. Ullman *op.cit.*, pp. 181-182.

be held individually responsible for anything that happened; but in spite of repeated invitations he declined to put his remarks into writing. The disarming of the Serbs and Italians was carried out quite quietly and without incident at midday.

"In the afternoon I received a visit from the Commander of *Alexander,* accompanied by his interpreter. He was extremely agitated. *Sviatogor*, he said, had come up the river in the morning and placed herself across the channel just below him. (It was found subsequently that she had merely fouled the channel, and had had to wait for the tide to float off). She had later passed up the river with a friendly wave of the hand from her Commander and had taken station with the trawlers, true to programme, up stream. Unfortunately the British Commander had got the idea into his head that he was going to be attacked or disarmed; and he had formed a hare-brained scheme of slipping his cable, ordering the *Egba* (the remaining British food-ship) to run on the mud north of the Maimaxa channel, and himself to make a run for it down to the bar and the White Sea. His position was not an easy one. His gun-power was quite inferior to that of *Sviatogor,* and he should never have been put in the position of having his bluff called. He knew nothing about Russia in general, or about the particular situation: and he refused to believe those who did. He declined to be reassured, and demanded that I should go round with him immediately to the Executive Committee and ask permission for his peaceful departure. I pointed out that, as we had refused a few weeks previously to withdraw the ship when asked by the Soviet authorities to do so, we should by acting as he desired place both ourselves and the British Government in a very humiliating position. Still he refused to be comforted.

"To risk his carrying out his plan of cutting and running would have meant to risk, if not the provoking of a small disaster, the explosion of the whole of Archangel in a roar of laughter at the British expense, just at the moment when it was most important for us to maintain our prestige. Accordingly I decided to go with him to the Executive Committee, where I put a rather hopeless case as delicately as I could. The first reply of the Vice-President was, as I expected, a broad grin, followed by an assurance that the Soviet authorities had, and had had, no intention of attacking *Alexander.* In return I gave the assurance that *Alexander* had no intention of attacking *Sviatogor*, and the situation immediately returned to the status quo.

"The British Commander, a very good fellow, had clearly 'got the wind up': and the whole thing was a typical instance of the evil results of the stupid policy of ignoring the Soviet authorities and attributing to them motives which did not exist. Captain Millson of the *Egba*, a hard-headed merchant skipper whose coolness and common sense had more than once contributed to ease the strain, had come into the Consulate in the morning to find out what was 'up', as he had received a signal from *Alexander* to be prepared to use his gun. (That signal, incidentally, was sent in the ordinary Morse Code, and was read and reported to the Consulate by a British civilian who happened to be strolling on the water-front. How many Bolshevik sailors read it, I do not know). When the situation was explained to him, he tumbled to it at once, and stated in the emphatic manner of his profession that he 'would be damned if he took part in any such nonsense'. He departed from the Consulate perfectly reassured, and watched the subsequent proceedings from a bench on the water-front, smoking a cigar.

"These are the facts of this incident, as I know them: and there are others in a position to confirm them. One could hardly have expected the Commander of *Alexander* to report in detail to the Senior Naval Officer, Murmansk, a joke against himself".

The reference in Young's narrative to the meeting of the British and French Consuls with the leaders of the Archangel Soviet is all too brief. A Soviet historian of intervention in the North, recounting the incident, remarked on Young's "much more correct" attitude at the interview, and wrote that he seemed embarrassed by the French Consul's outburst.[107] However, among Young's papers is the official record of the conversation, sent to both foreign Consuls; and it contains a further illustration of those peculiar defects in the attitude of many Allied officials towards the Soviet authorities which Young mentioned — as well as of his own careful and responsible attitude. After quoting the explanation by Vinogradov, a member of the Presidium of the Archangel Regional Executive Committee, why it was proposed that the Serbian soldiers should be disarmed and, together with the unarmed Italians, withdrawn from Archangel, it stated that "Mr. French Consul" was asked whether he would instruct them to conform to this decision. It continued:

"Mr. French Consul states the following: in the statement just made I see distrust of my State, offensive and unjustified by our past brotherhood in arms. I do not understand whether you have separated from your Central Government or not, because your insstructions are at variance with the instructions of the Central Government. From the fact that such a statement has been made to me, am I to conclude that you have separated? But in addition I must ask you, where is your boasted Russian hospitality, if you

107. Kedrov, *op. cit.*, pp. 51-52.

are sending back defenceless and exhausted people, anxious to return to their native country, thereby condemning them to further suffering? But I am sure that you and we are people guided by humanity in our actions. So I think that in this instance you will help them to return to their own country. Also I consider that, if you allow Mirbach (the German Ambassador after the Treaty of Brest-Litovsk *A.R.)* to come to Moscow — even if it is because you are defenceless — you will also allow those who are under my protection to leave for their country. They represent no danger to you, because the Allied Governments don't intend to consider you to be 'children who don't know how to behave'. I can say on behalf also of my British colleague that we have no intention of laying down the law here. In conclusion, I am authorised to declare on behalf of my Government the following (i) the disarmament of the armed soldiers under my protection I even consider necessary, but on condition of the observance of the telegram you have had from your Government that the arms must remain in the custody of their officers and sentries. But if, contrary to my expectations, events take place in the city which reveal inhumanity on your part, you will be judged by a tribunal which — like the laws under which you will be prosecuted — will be determined by circumstances of a political nature (the latter statement made with strong emphasis *A.R.*).

"Comrade Vinogradov puts the question: should your statement, Mr. Consul, be understood in the sense that you regard us not as the due authority, but as individuals answering for our actions individually, before whatever laws there may be? Mr. Consul replies: our Government has not recognised your Government, therefore we cannot regard you in the way you ask.

"Comrade Vinogradov puts the question: when you talk of a tribunal, have you in view an international court of arbitration? Mr. Consul replies: yes, that court too, but also a different court. Mr. Consul explained his words by the following example: if Chairman Popov were to find himself in France, he would answer for his actions under French law before a French court.

"Conrade Vinogradov says: after the massacre of Armenians in Turkish Armenia, the Allied Governments — including the Russian Government — officially declared to the Turkish Government that all the Turkish authorities individually, according to the orders they have issued, would answer for their actions according to the laws of each country in whose name this declaration was made to the Turkish Government. Is not your present statement, Mr. French Consul, analagous to that declaration of the Allied Governments to the Turkish? Mr. Consul confirms that the two statements are analagous.

"To the question put to Mr. Consul, whether comrades Vinogradov and Popov would be judged as individuals, and before what court, Mr. Consul replies: both Chairman Popov and Vinogradov would be judged by a court, the form of which would be determined by circumstances of a political nature, and — as he said previously — unquestionably as individual persons.

"On behalf of the Regional Executive Committee comrade Vinogradov states: in our decisions, Mr. French Consul, we are guided by principles of what is beneficial to the State, and no fear of personal responsibility can influence the decision of a revolutionary.

"We are a revolutionary authority, and have no fear of such responsibility. Moreover we as a revolutionary authority are not capable of inhumanity towards the persons under your protection, who are representatives of the Italian and Serbian poor. But if the interests of the State require the use of the most decisive measures, we shall not hesitate to apply them. We are not sending the persons under your protection to the Germans, but only to that place in the Russian Soviet Federative Republic whence they came. In the name of the Regional Executive Committee I emphatically insist on the disarmament of the persons under your protection and on their immediate despatch from Archangel.

"Any non-fulfilment of the present statement may lead to the most painful consequences, and the Regional Executive Committee places all responsibility for those consequences on you.

"Mr. French Consul puts the question, has the port of Archangel ceased to be open to French ships?

"Comrade Vinogradov explains that with the introduction of a state of war in the Archangel region free entry into the Archangel port has been prohibited. Vessels will be admitted to the inner basin of the river Dvina only by distinct permission of a special Commissioner.

"Comrade Vinogradov recalls that time is precious, and once again officially asks whether Mr. French Consul will give an instruction to the people under his protection unconditionally to obey the Archangel authorities. Mr. French Consul, rising, says that he can give no instructions, and with the words: 'Let that happen which must happen', leaves the meeting.

"Comrade Vinogradov, apologising to the British Consul, says that Mr. Consul was invited because the Regional Executive Committee was convinced that the decisions of the French and British Governments were identical, and asks, is Mr. British

Consul in agreement with the statements of Mr. French Consul?

"Mr. Consul Douglas Young says that he has no authority from his Government on the present question, but presumes that his Government may be in agreement with the French Government. Further Mr. British Consul enquires about the further destiny of peaceful British subjects living in the city of Archangel, and says that among them there is anxiety about what is to happen.

"Comrade Vinogradov states that it is proposed to free the city of all who are not indispensable: for example, it was decided to begin with the evacuation of the Serbo-Slavs and the Italians, which would be followed by all civilians at Archangel, including Russians.

"*Signed:* Stepan Popov, Chairman: Vinogradov and Jan Ozolin, Members of Presidium: Plastinina, Secretary".[108]

The French Consul's attempts at browbeating, not to speak of his hazardous excursions into international jurisprudence, were none the less characteristic of a wide-spread school of thought among Allied officials involved in preparation for intervention (of which another striking example still nearer home will be found in later pages). And they could not present a greater contrast with the restraint and diplomatic tact of Douglas Young on this occasion.

Next, Young recorded in his unpublished memoir a series of interviews which the Senior Naval Officer, Admiral Kemp, had himself with the Vice-President of the Archangel Soviet (Pavlin Vinogradov), at which Young was present, by special request of the Soviet authorities in consideration of his status. He wrote: "The meetings were perfectly friendly and marked with every courtesy on both sides. In fact, one is bound in justice to the Soviet officials to admit that in the matter of straight forwardness, outspokenness and respect for their undertakings they were a refreshing contrast to the slippery or prickly officials so characteristic of the old régime".

Kemp had on July 1 sent the British cruiser *Attentive* from Murmansk to Kem in the White Sea, in order to cooperate with the

---

108. The minute of these most remarkable proceedings, signed by Plastinina, is dated July 2, 1918. It is only appropriate and fair to mention here that the summary printed in one Soviet work — *The Struggle for the Soviets in the North (1918-1919)*, published in Russian at Archangel in 1926 — was based on a newspaper account, and does an injustice to Young by appearing to make him join in his French colleague's bluster.

In his own account, dictated to a stenographer in November, 1919, Young added that "Vinogradov plainly asked the French Consul if he really thought that he was going to frighten them with his threats, they who suffered in Tsarist prisons every possible provocation and outrage." Young noted also, as Kedrov did, that Plastinina (herself a professional revolutionary since 1904) asked the Frenchman if he would sign her minute of what he had said, and — when he refused — asked him if he would write the minute of his statement himself. He said he would do so on returning to his Consulate —but never did!

British troops then moving towards that town. Young wrote:

"At his first interview on July 5, the S.N.O., at the invitation of the Vice-President of the Soviet, proceeded to make a full and candid statement as to the objective of the Allied forces in the Murmansk district. He declared emphatically that their movements were not directed against the Bolsheviks but against possible German-Finnish attacks from the west. The Vice-President cross-examined the S.N.O in an extremely able manner, and obtained from him an emphatic assurance that no Allied naval movements could take place, during his absence from Murmansk, without his authority.

"Such was the effect of the S.N.O.'s statement and assurances, which certainly bore the impression of the complete honesty, that on the following morning the Vice-President requested me by telephone to go round to see him; and he then informed me that, on his report to the Executive Committee concerning the interview of the previous afternoon, it had been decided to meet the Allied representatives in regard to a matter which had resulted in deadlock hitherto.

"That matter had been discussed on the previous morning at a solemn meeting of British 'experts' — diplomatic, economic and naval. Owing to the fact that neither the newly-arrived Diplomatic Commissioner (Mr. Lindley *A.R.*) nor the Head of the Economic Mission (Sir William Clark, an official of the Department of Overseas Trade *A.R.*)[109] could speak a single word of Russian, the British side of the proceedings was conducted by Mr. Leslie Urquhart (owner in Tsarist days of big mining concessions in Siberia *A.R.*) whose sleek appearance and cynical manner effectively put the Soviet back up inside five minutes. The trouble was about the Allied refugees, who wished to leave for Murmansk and could not do so unless the Soviet authorities provided the necessary shipping. The latter declined to render this service unless the British, in return, agreed to hand over, against payment, the cargoes of the two food-ships which had been intended originally for exchange with munitions, and which had been lying undischarged on the port for more than two months. The British Commissioner rather pompously declared that public opinion in England would not tolerate what he chose to regard as a bargain with British subjects, and demanded the unconditional despatch of the British refugees.

"The result was a deadlock when the Diplomatic Mission

109. The Mission was on its way back to England, having spent exactly two days in Moscow (Ullman, op. cit., pp. 232-233).

departed. The matter was now arranged to our satisfaction, the Vice-President merely asking in return that their request should be considered on its merits. It is only fair to the naval diplomatist to admit that, in this case at any rate, he proved superior to his professional colleagues, even in methods.

"At the same or a subsequent interview the Vice-President put the S.N.O. through a cross-examination worthy of a smart London barrister. He had evidently heard something disturbing, and as the interrogation proceeded it became clear that he was fully informed about movements of Allied ships of war. He drew from the S.N.O. a list of the ships on the White Sea station, after obtaining a renewal of the assurance that no ship could move without the authority of the S.N.O. The latter gave them all — with the single and significant exception of *Attentive*. Then the Vice-President called his bluff on this point. The S.N.O. was too wise by this time to attempt dissimulation or prevarication, and fell back on the assurance that *Attentive* had been sent into the White Sea to cover the operations of the army against the prospective German-Finns. On the Vice-President's asking whether the ultimate objective of *Attentive* might be eastward to Onega (from which port there was a road by which a landing party could cut the railway line between Archangel and Vologda) the S.N.O. like Peter denied it thrice. It is fair to state that the S.N.O. added that 'he could not answer for Archangel', a statement which did not appear, under the circumstances, to astonish the Vice-President.

"Nevertheless the relations of the S.N.O. with the Vice-President became so cordial that one fine day, without any warning, he blurted out: 'I think the British Government ought to recognise the Soviet Government', and, turning to me in his impetuous way, he added: 'Don't you think so, Consul?' Respect for the truth compels me to confess that on this point the S.N.O. was away ahead of me. He had as usual been entirely secretive about his political, or diplomatic, education. Consequently, I was so utterly dumbfounded that I could only mumble something about recognising them as one would recognise a shower of rain".

But on July 17 Young reported the sharp change in the situation. He cabled to London: "Since July 11 telegrams from Murmansk and District have been refused, and S.S. communication stopped, owing to substantial reports of high-handed action by the British in the Kem district i.e. seizing of Russian ships and shooting of three members of Kem Soviet. Admiral Kemp and representatives of Archangel Soviet left to investigate. H.M. Ship *Alexander* sailed for Murmansk July

12".[110] In his unpublished memoir Young went on:

> "On the afternoon of July 11 I received an urgent request to go round to the Executive Committee of the Soviet, where I found the S.N.O. accompanied by the Commander of the British Naval icebreaker. There was clearly something wrong, for smiles were replaced by scowls on the faces of the Vice-President and the two other members who were with him. With considerable control of his feelings, the Vice-President informed us that the Committee has just received reliable information that Russian ships had been seized at Kem, the Soviet dispersed and three members of the Kem Soviet shot by Allied troops. The S.N.O. seemed to be as taken aback as I was. He immediately offered to take representatives of the Archangel Soviet across to Kem on his yacht in order to make an investigation. The invitation was declined, the Soviet representatives preferring to go on their own ship. The two vessels left on the following day, accompanied by the British naval icebreaker, which the S.N.O. himself now decided to withdraw. Even under the provocation of the incidents reported from Kem, the Soviet authorities did not go back on their undertaking in regard to the departure of the Allied refugees, requiring only a guarantee from the British authorities that two Russian ships furnished for their transport to Kandalaksha should be returned to Archangel in due course. The refugees left without incident at the same time as the naval party".

Young added (in a memorandum dictated in November, 1919) that he "told the Executive Committee that he entirely agreed with their description of it (the shooting *A.R.*) as an unwarrantable outrage".

What had happened at Kem has been partially described by American historians.[111] It may be summarised as follows. On the plea that a short raid by Finnish Whites towards Kem (disavowed by the Finnish Government in a message to the British Government) had taken place early in April, the Allied forces at Murmansk — with the approval of the local Soviet, whose Menshevik and Socialist-Revolutionary majority had already fallen away from Moscow — sent British, French and Serbian troops and an armoured train to Kandalaksha, eighty miles south of Murmansk ("a considerable distance inland", in Mr. Kennan's words). Then, in mid-May, the Kandalaksha railwaymen, supported by the workers at Kem, demanded the withdrawal of the Allied forces, and a group of Red Guards (armed workmen) were sent to the area from Petrograd to takes over defences from the now openly rebellious Murmansk Soviet.

---

110. F.O. 371, vol. 3330, p. 226.

111. E.g. Kennan, *op. cit.*, pp. 251-256, 260, 372-373; Ullman, *op. cit.*, pp. 175, 184.

General Maynard, commanding the Allied forces, planted machine-guns in the way of the first train of Red Guards, ordered it not to proceed, and finally disarmed the whole detachment. He then went on to Kem, where his troops broke up the District Soviet, arrested seven of its leaders and shot three of them — including the President Massorin, Vice-President Kamenev and secretary Yezhov. Two accounts of the affair reached the authorities in London much later. One, in a cable from Maynard to the War Office, stated: "While the Bolsheviks at Kem were being disarmed, three prominent citizens offered armed resistance with bombs and revolver, and during the struggle were unfortunately killed. We hold about 100 Bolsheviks who plotted against the Allies or the (Murmansk) Soviet detailed under guard". The other, in a cable from Maynard to Poole at Archangel, ran: "I ordered the disarming of the Red Guards at Kem on July 2 and a search for arms. During the search a house was entered in which the local Soviet was sitting. The members leapt to their feet. Two of them drew out their revolvers and one fired on the Serbians who were carrying out the search. Another threw a bomb which did not explode. During the struggle which ensued three members were shot".[112]

The Serbs carrying out the disarmament of the Red Guards were at battalion strength. The verisimilitude of the two accounts by General Maynard may be weighed against that printed in the Archangel Communist paper on July 17, 1918, which said that the three were "led out of the town and a volley was fired at them": the statement of a Serbian who deserted to the Soviet side that he had seen them, after arrest, taken on to the beach and shot there: and the fact that by a peculiar coincidence the three members shot were precisely the principal officials of the Soviet.[113]

In any case, it obviously did not occur to General Maynard that his acts of war against Red Guards and the local authorities in a Russian town were taking place in a country with which Britain was nominally at peace, or that Russians whom he arrested because they were "plotting against the Allies" were acting in defence of their country and under the orders of their Government, whom the British authorities had repeatedly assured that they did not intend to intervene in Russian internal affairs. The general state of mind of senior British officers on the spot was well illustrated by an extract from letters by Lieut.-Cdr. H.E. Rendall which appeared in the ultra-respectable Cornhill Magazine (1919, p. 414): "(There was) a sort of monarchical uprising in Kem. Fortunately the three biggest scound-

---

112. F.O. 371, vol. 3335, cables of August 14 and September 1, 1918.

113. *Arhangelskaya Pravda,* 17 July, 1918: and a letter of M.M. Litvinov to the Foreign Secretary (F.O. 371, vol. 3335, under date August 21, 1918).

rels in the place were shot".

The report of the Soviet delegates who had visited Kem was published in the Archangel press on July 24th. It stated that the charges levelled against the Allied military command had been correctly reported. Young wrote in his unpublished memoir:

"They were not even denied: but the shooting of the three members of the Kem Soviet was 'explained' on the conventional plea of 'resisting arrest'. It appeared that the victims were arrested by the Serbs, encouraged to attempt to escape and then shot down. During their stay at Kem the Soviet delegates were confined by the Allied command to their train, under a guard of Serbian soldiers".

The armed assault on Archangel was now very near. Young could have had only a hint of the Foreign Office and War Office correspondence in which during recent months the preparation had been so thoroughly discussed. But the events on the Murman coast left him in very little doubt, quite apart from the French Consul's confident assertion a month before. His own position was becoming more and more distasteful. For example, he had had to issue a "certificate" of identity to Chaplin (the camouflaged Russian officer) when the latter lost his *false* British passport, issued in Petrograd. Moreover things were made worse by what Young in his memoirs called the "amazing indiscretions" of the conspirators, both Russian and Allied. It is interesting that Mr Kennan also writes of British efforts, during the last weeks of July, 1918, "with vigour and urgency, through secret agents, to stimulate an uprising by the anti-Communist forces at Archangel, to be coordinated with the arrival of an Allied landing force... The fact that they were taking place remained no great secret from the Soviet authorities".[114]

After the Allied Ambassadors had passed through Archangel at the end of the month, Young had delivered to him letters which they had left behind with a doorkeeper for the Consulate. One proved to have come from Capt. Cromie, "and the contents were such, if they had fallen into the hands of the Russian authorities, as to give the whole show away and hang the lot of us".

Nevertheless, Young wrote, "even after the provocative action of the Allied military in the Murman district, there was not so much as a hostile demonstration against the Allied Consulates. In the very last days, when the Allied intentions were no longer in doubt, the British Naval Transport Office was searched for concealed weapons... Fortunately the Acting P.N.T.O. was an elderly and hard-headed merchant captain who kept to his legitimate business, turned in disgust from the contemptible foolery of the military and had no taste for the theatrical".

114. *Op. cit.*, p. 424.

In his later memoir, Young wrote that he had intended to resign at this point, but that his American colleague Cole persuaded him not to do so.

By this time the Allied diplomats, who had originally taken refuge at Vologda at thc end of February, 1918, from an imaginary German menace to Moscow, had on July 25 left hurriedly for Archangel, again supposing that they were to be either handed over to the Germans or detained as hostages for the Allied invasion known to be coming. Very soon after their arrival, on the night of July 28-29, they withdrew once more — on ships provided by the Soviet authorities — to Kandalaksha, which they reached on July 30.

There is a very well-known version of why they left for the protection of the Allied military on the Murman coast. It was given by U.S. Ambassador Francis to a Senate Committee: "We had determined to leave for Kandalaksha because there was an anti-Bolshevik revolution to be pulled off at Archangel, and we knew it, and we did not want to be there when it occurred, and they knew it." [115]

Mr Lindley, in a confidential report to the Foreign Secretary a few days later, was far more explicit. Directly the party arrived at Kandalaksha, he said, he had informed General Poole, who was at Murmansk, that the long delay in occupying Archangel was causing a deplorable effect. "A rising had been arranged at Archangel to take place at 3 a.m. on July 31, and the Allied military officers acquainted with the plan were absolutely confident that the town would be in the hands of our friends without bloodshed, and in the course of a few hours after the first move had been made. This move had already been postponed several times; and the result was that many people connected with it had been arrested by the Bolsheviks, and not a few shot. It was impossible for this to continue." Although quite confident of initial success, the leaders were not sure that they would be able to hold out unless quickly supported from outside. Lindley "therefore did all in my powers to urge Gen. Poole to come into Archangel within 48 hours of the fall of the Bolsheviks. Gen. Poole replied that all his arrangements had been made for a later date, and it was absolutely impossible for him to advance that date to a day before August 6." Lindley expressed deep concern at this decision, and reported it to the Allied Representatives. They felt the results would be disastrous, and decided to leave for Murmansk that night in order to bring pressure to bear personally on the General. However during the afternoon Lindley received a further message from Gen. Poole that he had reconsidered the matter, and that he was starting

---

115. Report and Hearings of the Sub-Committee on the Judiciary, U.S. Senate, 65th Congress, document no. 62, p. 949.

immediately with all the forces at his disposal. Lindley's colleagues were "exceedingly gratified" at this change of plan.[116]

In a further report to Lord Curzon, on his work from June, 1918 to March, 1919, Mr. Lindley added that when he was in Archangel he "had several consultations with Major McGrath and Mr Harrison, who were working for Gen. Poole in the town. They informed me that Chaplin, a Russian naval officer, had made all his preparations to turn out the Soviet and replace it by a pro-Allied government". But he was "in despair" at the frequent postponements of the Allied landing, because "he could not be sure of holding his own for more than a few days against forces sent from outside".

When the diplomats did leave, "Mr. Consul Young decided to remain at his post, and Mrs. Young refused to leave her husband." [117]

Young wrote of these final days in his memoir:

> "As for the 'revolution' which (Mr. Francis so carelessly reveals) had to be 'pulled off' at Archangel, it was a non-local and purely artificial movement, from the naval officer who was sent from Petrograd to organise it to the military and Socialist-Revolutionary groups who quarrelled over the power when the Allied forces put it into their hands. It was just a put-up job between the Moscow White Guard and the Allied Missions. There were plenty of well-to-do people, anxious for their properties or bank balances, who would gladly have put the Bolsheviks to slow torture — if only the Allies would pinion the intended victim during the operation. But the anti-Bolshevik movement, outside the small officer clique, was as an active force as big a myth as the 'loyal' or 'anti-German' tale about the same White Russians. The Russian masses were grumbling, and would have continued to grumble against any Government that failed to work the miracle of restoring pre-war economic conditions by a stroke of the pen. But the classes skulking behind the White Guard movement were even more afraid for their skins than for their possessions."

It will be seen that the analysis made by Young practically coincided with that given by the American Vice-Consul in the despatch of June 1 quoted earlier. Meanwhile, Young persuaded his wife on July 30 to gather as many of the British civilians as she could reach, so that they could quietly make their way to a village six miles distant.

Under the pressure from the Allied diplomats described so fully in Mr Lindley's despatch, Gen. Poole and Admiral Kemp literally did scrape together a few hundred men, and set off for Archangel with a small armada. According to Mr. Lindley (in the narrative of April 25, 1919, just quoted), the latter consisted of the French cruiser *Aube*

116. F.O. 175, Box 7, report dated August 5, 1918.

and the British light cruiser *Attentive,* a seaplane ship *Nairana*, Admiral Kemp's yacht, two Russian destroyers taken over by the British and a transport. Young wrote: "The expedition was saved from probable disaster by a fog and a piece of fine navigation by a young officer of *Attentive,* which brought the Allied ships through the 'throat' of the White Sea unobserved by the signal stations along either shore; and the first thing the Archangel authorities knew about it was the news, received late on the night of July 31, that Allied ships of war had bombarded Onega and landed troops." It was only on this news that, Young wrote, the Allied Consuls were briefly detained in their own Consulates. "The plan to cut the Archangel-Vologda railway at Obozerskaya failed, owing to the resistance of the Reds; but the Allied squadron bombarded the battery at Mudyug, off the entrance to the Northern Dvina river, with gunfire and air bomb. The battery was not silenced before it had burst a shell in the forward funnel of *Attentive*, just above the bridge. A seaplane from the *Nairana* flew over the town. The Bolsheviks were taken completely by surprise; and to add to the apparent good luck of the Allies, the special Commissar Kedrov, who had been sent from Moscow to take charge of the Archangel district, happened to have left for the capital to make a personal report. The Bolshevik organisation was honeycombed with agents of the White Guards, who had taken important posts with the deliberate intention of betraying the Bolsheviks, and the latter evacuated in a momentary panic." [117]

As for the supposed rising, Young wrote that there was none whatsoever, for the simple reason that it would have had no chance of success. "After the Allied attack had scared the Bolsheviks out of the town, the mock 'invitation' to the Allies to enter was sent in duplicate by the rival claimants to power — by M. Chaikovsky on the one hand, and on the other by a worthless gang of officers of the famous 'wild division', whose first act after the flight of the Bolsheviks was to seize the safe at military headquarters and divide several million roubles of public monies among themselves."

---

117. The same picture in essentials, and with much greater detail, was drawn by M.S. Kedrov, the special commissioner sent by the Soviet Government in May, 1918, whom Young mentioned, in his *Za Sovetski Sever* ("For a Soviet North"), Leningrad, 1927, pp. 95-97, 104-105, 114-121. One of Young's remarks moreover is well illustrated by a despatch from Petrograd via Stockholm to Admiral Kemp at Murmansk, with a copy to Gen. Poole, presumably sent by Capt. Cromie: "Col. Speranski, sent by the Bolsheviks as Chief of Staff for (Petrozavodsk region), is an officer of Chaplin's organisation and well known to me. He will arrange points for passing recruits for the North, and will command the brigade mentioned by .... as wishing to turn over to us on arrival at the front. I attach great importance to this officer, and am in touch with local draft officers that this brigade be sent to Petrozavodsk" (F.O. 371, vol. 3307, dispatch dated August 8, 1918).

Mr. Lindley, in a despatch confirming the precipitate departure of the Soviet forces when Allied planes flew over the city on August 1, continued with an eloquent admission: "*As soon as the Bolsheviks departed*, the movement which was originally intended to take place some days before the arrival of the Allies broke out, and in a few hours our friends were masters of the town... The course of events has shown pretty clearly that if our Russian friends had as originally intended risen some days before the arrival of the Allies, Kedrov and his mercenaries would in all probability have succeeded in disposing of them before we could come in. This is a contingency which I feared when I passed through Archangel a fortnight ago, and I then strongly advised those who were in touch with the movement not to allow it to break out before they were absolutely certain of Allied support reaching them within a few hours... There is no doubt that a great number of Bolsheviks are still left among the factory hands." [118]

The initial success of the invasion (which, Young wrote, bore more than a superficial resemblance to the notorious Jameson Raid) did not last. "Within a few days the Soviet troops, recovering from their initial panic and receiving reinforcements from the south, turned and held up, until the end of the story, the Allied forces which had advanced little more than one quarter of the distance to Vologda," wrote Young.

Describing the invasion itself a month later (September 10) Felix Cole reported to the State Department that the crowd welcoming the foreign troops was composed entirely of the bourgeoisie and the wealthier peasantry. "The working class was patently absent... During the march of the Allied officers through the streets to the Government building, the absence of the working class was even more conspicuous." [119] Their obvious distrust was soon given substantial support by the actions of the new authorities. General Poole immediately proclaimed martial law and appointed a French officer, Col. Donop, military commandant of the town, while the "moderate Socialist" government of Mr. Chaikovsky appointed Capt. Chaplin "Commander of the Armed Forces of the Supreme Government of the Northern Region." Among the orders issued during the first few weeks were abolition of workers' control in the factories (August 13), restoration of the respective Tsarist flags for warships and mercantile marine (August 14), reintroduction of courts martial and the death penalty (August 30), return of nationalised shipping to its previous owners (September 2) and cancellation of all Soviet decrees regarding social insurance (September 13). By September 9 Gen. Poole's régime had aroused such

118. F.O. 175, Box 7, despatch of August 15, 1918.

119. Quoted by Ullman *op. cit.*, p. 236.

concern in Washington that the Secretary of State told the British Ambassador that, if there was no change, the United States would seriously consider withdrawing its troops from Poole's command. In an angry but revealing response (September 15) the General promised to modify his methods in agreement with Mr. Lindley (now High Commissioner), but declared: "It would be absolutely fatal to the success of military operations to allow freedom of speech and propaganda to the Bolsheviks... Here amongst the working classes Bolshevism has many devoted adherents." He objected to "a free hand being allowed to a government which is afraid of them and panders to them": it would lead to "riots, incendiarism and strikes". In fact a military coup engineered by Chaplin on September 5, with the tacit consent of Gen. Poole, displaced the Chaikovsky Government for 24 hours. But it led to a general strike of workmen and the arrival of detachments of armed peasants in the town, which added a decisive argument to the United States Ambassador's successful protest and produced the reinstatement of Chaikovsky, although with a new government in which business elements were strongly represented.[120]

By this time, however, Young had left Archangel for good. He tried, he wrote subsequently, to discuss the futility of the occupation with Mr. Lindley, even before it took place. But Lindley took little interest and, seeing that the task was "a hopeless one", Young had applied for leave as early as July 4. On July 8 Lindley had in fact cabled that Young was in need of leave "owing to long strain", but no reply came. Now, on August 9, Lindley again cabled that Young's health required it: and on August 19 his assistant Saunders cabled that Mr. and Mrs. Young had sailed on the 17th by the *Egba* — the food-ship which had been lying undischarged for several months. On its way back to England it was run into and badly holed by a U.S. minelayer at 2 a.m., 60 miles off the Orkneys.

It remains to be added that, with later reinforcements, the Allied forces at Archangel by March 26, 1919, numbered 13,100 British, 4,820 Americans, 2,349 French, 1,340 Italians and 1,280 Serbs — with 11,770 Russians mobilised by the Archangel Government. The figures were given on that date to the Chamber of Deputies in Paris by Foreign Minister Pichon.

Young's condition was not only prompted by his rejection of the policy of occupation. Among his papers there is a certificate, dated September 27, 1918, by the Professor of Medicine in the University of Edinburgh, to the effect that Young was suffering from dyspepsia and nervous exhaustion, with recurrent boils, and required at least two months' leave.

120. F.O. 175, Box 7 cables of September 9, 13 and 15, 1918.

PART IV

12

In his unpublished memoir, Young wrote: "I left Archangel on the first ship to sail from that port after the occupation, and, arriving in London on the last day of August, I was the first British official, if not the first Allied subject, to reach England after the commencement of hostilities, an event which had been preceded by two or three weeks of complete interruption even of telegraphic communication with the West". In fact, even postal communication between Archangel and England had been suspended in effect for six months. Still subject to certain illusions about the Government's policy — in particular, being ignorant of the War Cabinet's decision of the previous December — Young hoped "to bring the real facts of the situation to the notice of His Majesty's Government. For apart from the fact that they were acting upon false assumptions, it was clear that much of our proceedings in Russia had been carried out without the knowledge or sanction of the Government, and were of such a nature as to involve it inevitably in embarrassing claims by the Soviet Government, in the event — which seemed to me a certainty — of the latter surviving our attempts to destroy them."

Accordingly, directly on arrival, Young repaired to the Foreign Office, and was conducted by a Consular colleague from Russia who was temporarily working there to see Sir George Clerk, the head of the Northern Department (which dealt with Russian affairs). Clerk had been a member of Lord Milner's mission to Russia in 1917. Young said: "In official gossip he is credited with two rather unusual claims to fame. He is said, on his arrival in Russia, to have mistaken a high Tsarist official of the reception party for a sleeping-car attendant, and to have called on him to produce shaving-water; and on his return to England to have signed, a few days before Tsardom tumbled to pieces, a minority report to the effect that the Russian nation was never more devoted to the Imperial throne!". Young's suggestion that a mistake had been made in Russia, and that things had been done in the name of Britain of which the Foreign Office was unaware — with the probability of "bitter disillusionment for the Allied Governments" — were met with an "ominous silence". Sir George brightened up when Young told him of a protest by Chaikovsky against the behaviour of the British military authorities, and asked for it to be put in writing. This Young did. The text of his statement, dated September 4, is worth quoting in full, not only because of its content, but also for the composure with which it was received at the Foreign Office — not to speak of the writer's still surviving illusions about Russian politics, illustrated by his final paragraphs.

"1. On the day of my departure from Archangel (August 16) Mons. Tchaikovski, Head of the Provisional Government, called on me, and in response to my request for a frank statement of his views regarding Allied activities in Archangel, he opened his heart.

"He claimed that a strong Russian civil authority in Archangel, sincerely supported by the Allies, was absolutely essential. The Provisional Govt. of which he was the head was composed of elected members of the Constituent Assembly for various Northern and North-Western Governments (Viatka, Archangel, Vologda, Novgorod, Kazan and Samara) and could consequently claim to have received a popular mandate. They were moreover delegated by their central party organisation.

"In spite of this, he said, 'the Allied military command (i.e. Gen. Poole) does not appear to realise the necessity, and loses no opportunity of either ignoring or weakening the prestige of the Russian Civil Authority'. A French military officer had been appointed by Poole to be Military Governor of Archangel, and this officer had for instance stopped the functioning of an Investigating Committee, appointed by the Provisional Government to examine the cases of the Bolshevik prisoners who had fallen into their hands before and after the Allied occupation.

"M. Tchaikovski complained that Poole failed to reply to a written request of his for an appointment to discuss certain matters, and no appointment had been made. 'Gen. Poole', he concluded, 'claimed to be the supreme authority in Archangel'.

"The lavish requirements of the Allied Military Command for office and dwelling accommodation in the town, which throughout had failed for practical reasons to meet the demands of an ever increasing influx of population, also worries the Provisional Govt., who are too polite to state frankly and firmly that the Allies must cut their coat in relation to the restricted supply of cloth. This is all the more regrettable as the Russian authorities in Archangel have throughout, even under the Tsarist régime, been conspicuous for the modesty of their private and official establishments. One of Gen. Poole's first acts was to requisition for himself and his personal staff the largest and finest private residence in the town, belonging to a sawmill owner who was a Russian subject. Even the Bolsheviks allowed the owners to occupy part of this house, but it was only after the owner's wife had told Gen. Poole that he was 'worse than the Bolsheviks' that they were allowed to retain four rooms. The same thing was evident in the innumerable departments of the Allied military organisation. Whole school buildings were requisitioned, and in large rooms capable of holding four or five people might be seen one officer and one table.

"Shortly after Gen. Poole's arrival certain orders were placarded in the streets, signed by him and beginning 'I forbid', e.g. the holding of meetings even in private houses, without 'my previous sanction', and the hoisting of any (Russian) flag except the emblem of the old régime. Even the Bolsheviks in their sunniest days were moderate in the use of the first personal pronoun when issuing orders. The Commander of H.M.S. *Attentive,* after having a private telephone cable run out of his ship in the stream, issued an order over his own signature stating that no vessel 'has the right' to anchor within certain limits.

"On August 14, in the third number of a new newspaper *Vozrozhdenie Severa* ('Resurrection of the North'), among whose sponsors and contributors are Tchaikovski and several members of the Provisional Govt. there appeared an anonymous article expressing disappointment with Gen. Poole's 'proclamation to the citizens of Russia' on the ground of indefiniteness and lack of sincerity. It closed by likening Allied action to a 'colonial policy... with this difference only that nothing is said to Africans about the possibility of choosing their own form of government'.

"According to my information, a French officer was sent round by Poole to see the Editor and demanded the name of the author, which was refused, and a stormy scene ensued.

" Mon. Tchaikovski also complained of an attempt of the Allied Military Command to seize a small reserve of paper, over the heads of the local authorities, for a newspaper (Russian) which Poole is anxious to launch and back financially, under the direction of Semenovich, whom Tchaikovski alleges to have been associated with the old *Novoye Vremya*, and therefore not of the political complexion desired by the Provisional Government." [121]

"2. The Allied Ambassadors reached Archangel on their return from the Murman coast only a week after the entry of the military, and consequently found the latter firmly established on the box seat. The Civil representative of H.M.G. has in any case

121. The old paper of that name was one of the staunchest official supporters of the monarchy.

been all along engaged in a hopeless 'struggle' (this unpleasant word unfortunately describes the situation) to retain direction of his legitimate functions, and to resist the encroachments, at first of the Admiralty and now of the War Office organisations, upon questions of a purely civil nature.

"I had already gathered from Gen. Poole's advance-guard that in their firm opinion the entire Allied organisation was to be controlled by Poole, and when, on the arrival of the expeditionary force, I drew Admiral Kemp on the subject of the probable return of the diplomatic corps, he replied: 'We will not let them come'.

"Although Mr. Lindley was my guest for the week which I remained in Archangel after his arrival, he did not confide in me (it is sad to relate that Archangel, now more than ever, offers an example of the unfortunate water-tight compartment system, rendering cooperation impossible owing to the three-ply barrier of service jealousy, departmental prejudices and personal ambition). I gathered however that in conjunction especially with the American Ambassador he was doing his best to secure fair play for the Provisional Government against the British military dictatorship. Even if he is successful, much valuable time will be lost in settling petty intrigues where close cooperation ought to exist. The only effective remedy would be to confine the functions of the Military Command to purely military affairs, leaving civil and economic questions to be settled by the Russian civil authority, with the sincere advice and support of the Allied Representatives and not their dictation.

"The military situation with the rapid approach of the bitter northern winter is sufficiently precarious to occupy the whole time of our military representatives, who are entirely fresh to the work. Moreover, there is the danger of the military command becoming the catspaw of the reactionaries and restorationists, which would be fatal to a lasting settlement in the north.

"The Provisional Govt. is doubtless far from perfect, and may need modification and the infusion of men of practical ability. But Allied action will best succeed not by backing one political party or class, but by endeavouring to reconcile parties and classes on the basis of a peasant bourgeois policy backed by energetic economic activity, which alone can satisfy the mass of the population.

Sept. 4th 1918

(signed) D. Young, H.B.M. Consul, Archangel".[122]

122. F.O. 371, vol. 3339, pp. 110-112.

The Foreign Office officials, certainly well aware that all round the Russian compass British military activity was taking place in the closest cooperation with "the reactionaries and restorationists", could merely take note of Young's complaint. "This record of military and naval indiscretions makes rather melancholy reading, but the Russians are no doubt fairly impossible to deal with" (E.H.C.); "the Secretary of State has already seen this report" (J.D. Gregory); and a simple endorsement: "H." — Lord Hardinge of Penshurst.

It is probable, indeed, that they were finding Young himself, with his illusions about British policy, "fairly impossible to deal with". For when, on presenting the above memorandum to Sir George Clerk, Young indicated to him "the peculiar circumstances which explained the raid on the former (Petrograd) Embassy building" and the shooting of Capt. Cromie (reported that morning in the press) — apart from the fact that Allied forces had opened hostilities without a declaration of war — Sir George was "as suggestively silent as at our first meeting". But when, on leaving (wrote Young), "I stated my innocent intention as soon as possible to send in the usual routine report on events of the past month, which I believe might help His Majesty's Government to get at the truth of the Russian situation, he anxiously and urgently deprecated the making of any report whatsoever". This surprised Young greatly: he could not understand why the mere possibility of a report not yet made, "should fill a responsible official of the Foreign Office with such alarm as to suggest that the report might be unsuitable even for tranquil repose in the secret pigeon-holes of that Department". On the one hand, he wrote, he had to assume that Clerk was speaking in the name of Mr Secretary Curzon; on the other hand, that the Secretary of State was not receiving information of importance.

At all events, Young at the time sent in no report, although he did prepare it for use if required. Its essence (as the document preserved in his papers shows) was that "agents of the British Military Command were allowed — with or without the sanction of His Majesty's Government — to enter into a dishonourable and dangerous intrigue with the anti-Soviet Russian factions, whose judgement was inevitably warped by self-interest and personal loss. The object of this intrigue, which was carried on under cover of diplomatic immunity, was to overthrow the de facto authority of a country whose official hospitality British representatives were enjoying", and to whom formal assurances had been given "that the Allied Governments had no intention of interfering in the internal affairs of Russia". Such methods, he said, "were not in accordance with truth and honest dealing".[123]

---

123. Statement to the Foreign Office prepared by Young, but sent in March 4, 1919.

Young was moreover incensed by the fact that throughout he had been given no clear guidance as to the policy which the Government was pursuing, and to the last he failed to obtain any indication that military intervention was intended. Indeed, as he bitterly wrote afterwards in his unpublished memoir: "When deciding to adopt Prussian methods, they (the British Government) might at least have sent out a confidential circular to harrassed and hardworking public servants, placed in the position of British representatives in Russia, informing them that official British statements about justice, honour, humanity, etc. were not to be taken seriously, as they were only intended for purposes of public propaganda."

Meanwhile, Young evidently felt free at last to press the Foreign Office on a more personal matter. He had had eleven years of service now, three of them at Archangel, where he still remained formally a Vice-Consul, with only a local rank as Consul, although he had been fulfilling the full duties of Consul with substantive rank and much higher pay. A man in uniform at Murmansk, "who dropped into his job from the skies" in 1916, had immediately been made full Consul, while Young remained exactly where he was three years ago.[124]

This letter, as usual in such cases, had some effect, and on October 25 Young entered upon temporary duties (for three or four months) in the Russian section of the Department of Overseas Trade, at a Consul's salary.

During the following weeks, while the end of the war with the Central Powers was rapidly approaching, the press campaign against Soviet Russia and in support of Allied intervention increased in violence. At the same time Young was receiving letters from his friends at Archangel which could only have added to his indignation, and possibly clarified his views. The following are typical extracts from the private letters of his acting Vice-Consul, G.D. Wiskemann.

> *August 21.* "Requisitioning of houses and rooms continues galore and causes considerable discontent... The greatest difficulty seems to be to find accommodation for the asses, with due respect to seniority."

> *September 9.* "Recruiting is poor, and quite obviously the majority of those who do join only do so to get food and clothing... The pukka bourgeois has done *nothing* to assist matters, now that his skin is temporarily safe and his bank balance looks a bit happier... Wages are freely cut down and rations issued in lieu. The 'bourjuika' is even more despicable than her husband. She regards the whole stunt as merely a nuisance, now that there is no more chocolate to be had at 60 roubles a piece, as the Y.M.C.A. can-

124. F.O. 369, vol. 1022, letter of September 23, 1918 to Sir W. Clark.

teen had to be closed in view of the most horrible 'spekulatsia' in this and other commodities".

September 18. "Cannot attempt to describe events since my last letter... It has been coups d'état and counter-coups d'état — strikes, vanishing governments and so on... One does not know from day to day whether there is a government or not — but it seems to make little difference either way. Kemp is having another shot at throwing out all Allied women and children, but I think I have put the lid on him... I have formed an Allied Burial Board to look after Cemetery and graves, but we find it difficult to keep pace with the daily provision of coffins — almost entirely unfortunate Yanks, who are dying like flies of this influenza business."

October 4. "For your own sake don't ever come back here, at any rate so long as this farce is on, and increasing every day... You never saw such a *kasha* (mess) in your life... We have been rushed off our feet with Spanish Flu, which has accounted for about 70 Yanks, quite outside ordinary casualties.".

November 3. "What a lot I could and should write — but I had better refrain I suppose. Suffice it to say that you are *very well* out of it... If they want you to go to Russia in the wake of another expedition, then make it the South and Odessa — where perhaps Nature will help them not to make such an unholy mess of it. You have no idea of what goes on. The latest is as follows: the new money has just arrived, beautifully printed, and every note large and small is literally covered with two-headed eagles and imperial crowns and actually monograms,[125] not to mention the usual coats of arms of all the old hangers-on — Finland, Poland, etc. What more perfect propaganda could old man Bolshie expect to be thrust in his hands. The powers that be are tearing their hair... Half the crew of nearly every ship is laid up, and on one 16 Lascars and 2 officers pegged out... I can tell you, it's overtime in the undertaking department, and the new cemetery will shortly be full up".

Felix Cole, now U.S. Consul and a prey to much the same illusions as Young, wrote in much the same strain on October 5. He said that the attempted military coups in September, after a month of occupation, had "effectually killed what enthusiasm for the Allies was left. A grand chance to make good with Russia — democratic Russia — was lost, and lost irretrievably". Government Ministers had wanted to resign, but he had argued them out of it: it would be "granting that the Bolsheviks were right about intervention". The Government

125. Of Nicholas II.

remained, but "despised by all and powerless, a poor camouflage for our 'occupation'... the only figleaf which the Allies had".

It was under the influence of such thoughts, and in the light of the wildest misstatements of the press about Soviet Russia, that Young (as he wrote) came to the conclusion "that His Majesty's Government were not in reality aware of the whole facts (the only alternative assumption was one which respect for H.M.G. and deference due from a subordinate official could not allow me for a moment to entertain)". He therefore decided to commit "a deliberate technical breach of discipline, in a form which appeared to be the surest and quickest way of attracting the attention of the Secretary of State."

No less ingenuous than his remark about the "deference" he owed to the Foreign Secretary was his first decision, according to an undated note in his handwriting, to offer the article he was planning to the *Daily Mail* — a newspaper which had been among the most virulent and hysterical champions of intervention up to that time. Only after he had written it, and it had been rejected, did he give it to the *Herald.* He was asked to do this by B.N. Langdon-Davies and W.N. Ewer, foreign editor of the *Herald,* both former Cambridge men like himself, whom he had met at the 1917 Club, founded by left-wing Socialists after the Russian Revolution. As such, these two were particularly interested in Young's story.

13

The article which Young wrote for the *Herald* is printed as a prologue to this book. It summed up the bewilderment, grief and indignation which had succeeded one another in his mind during the painful months of 1918.

No British daily paper had the courage to comment on Young's article or even mention it. Even Liberal newspapers which were criticising intervention, like the *Manchester Guardian,* the *Westminster Gazette,* the *Daily News* and its evening companion *The Star*, did not refer to the *Herald* article in their almost daily attacks on the Allied policy towards Russia. This was natural in the prevailing conditions, when the press was still very conscious of war-time Defence Regulations, and even more because all of them were supporting the Tories, the Coalition Liberals or the Asquithian Liberals in the election, and feared an adverse effect on their votes if they publicised such a "subversive" document. The same unquestionably applied to the "respectable" weeklies like the *New Statesman* — which mildly criticised intervention — or the *Spectator,* which strongly supported it.

Only the two chief Socialist weeklies reported Young's action. The *Labour Leader,* organ of the Independent Labour Party, did so the following week (December 19). Under the title "Restoring Order in Russia", it quoted extensively from Young's article. In a savage editorial comment, Philip Snowden wrote: "Our Government are in league with all the reactionary elements in Russia, and the only purpose of our occupation is to overthrow a Government supported by the vast majority of the Russian people, because that Government is not one of a character which commends itself to the financial and propertied classes of the Allied countries... The British Government and its Allies are writing a chapter of history which will be one of the most disgraceful ever recorded". *The Call*, organ of the British Socialist Party, quoted Young's article on its front page, with an accompanying comment couched in equally strong terms, by one of the B.S.P. leaders, E.C. Fairchild. Sylvia Pankhurst's *Workers' Dreadnought*, which had for long been opposing intervention, nevertheless maintained its sectarian peculiarity by attacking the *Herald* (for its "anti-Socialist" policy) and not mentioning Young's article.

The latter had of course been noticed by the Foreign Office officials. A telegram from Mr. Lindley at Archangel to Sir Eric Drummond ran: "I have just seen a misleading and objectionable article in *The Herald* of December 14 by Consul Douglas Young, late of Archangel. Can you tell me where he is now?" A reply came to him from Lord Curzon: "Mr Young has been instructed to furnish an explanation of the article in question, pending the receipt of which he has been suspended from the service. Letters in *The Times* were also written by him in the issues of December 19 and January 6." [126]

The shock caused by the article in the *Herald* had in fact been overtaken by the much greater uproar caused in official quarters by an exchange of letters between Admiral Kemp and Douglas Young in *The Times.* A general election was due in just over a fortnight. On December 13, 1918 *The Times*, which was naturally in the front rank of the interventionists, had printed an article by Kemp expressly written because of "the coming elections" and "the fact that a considerable section in the Labour Party are demanding non-intervention and the withdrawal from North Russia of Allied troops."

---

126. F.O. 175, Box 2, cables of January 9 and 25, 1919.

Kemp stated that "many thousands of Allied subjects were flying for their lives from the anarchy in the interior", while Murmansk was "menaced by a German-Finnish attack". The "de facto Government of the Russian Republic" had initially approved Allied intervention. When the Central Government changed its attitude, "probably under German pressure", the provincial authorities repudiated their allegiance and "threw in their lot with the Allies": this "rendered inevitable the forcible occupation of Archangel." The Soviet Government "had virtually declared war with the Allies". Allied subjects in large numbers had been imprisoned, shockingly ill treated and in many cases formally sentenced to death, while the British Naval Attaché had been murdered "by the organised military force of the Russian Republic". Access to Archangel, on the verge of famine, had been "denied to Allied ships", while the Soviet Government had sold "hundreds of thousands of tons" of coal and war material to the Germans "to be used against the Allies on the Western front". Now intervention had secured to the people of the occupied territories "the blessing of ordered government under a Russian National Administration".

Kemp demanded the occupation of Kronstadt, Petrograd and Moscow, and "the surrender to the Allies of Lenin, Trotsky, Tchitcherin and the principal commissaries responsible for the orgy of outrage and massacre in Russia", as part of the "forcible smash-up of Bolshevism". He claimed that, having served continuously in Russia from 1915 to 1918, he was "closely in touch with current events".

In their essence Kemp's allegations reflected no more than attacks on the Bolsheviks repeated for months past in the British press. But his final sentence had the effect of stinging Young into action the very next day. His reply was printed by *The Times* on December 19.

He challenged Kemp's claim to know anything about Archangel under the Bolshevik regime: the Admiral left the city on December 17, 1917 and — except for a few days in July — did not return until the arrival of the Allied expeditionary force on August 2. He, Young, claimed to be the only British official competent to express an authoritative opinion on the whole period at Archangel from December 17 to August 7.

He suggested that the attitude of the Soviet Government might have changed "because we had allowed ourselves to drift from an anti-German policy to a policy obviously anti-Soviet". He pointed out that British subjects had been imprisoned and Cromie murdered not before the occupation, but more than a month later: in fact that the position of the British even in Moscow, as Lockhart's own secretary had stated, "was not made uncomfortable until August 4". Young went on to assert that there was a considerable body of opinion in

Britain which felt that "our dealings with the Soviet Government do not accord with the British tradition of fair play and honest treatment". In particular, the actions of "certain British representatives in Russia" gave the Soviet "good grounds for suspecting us of deceiving them and of playing a deliberate double game". As an example, he reminded Kemp that on July 6, 1918, in Young's presence, he had assured the Archangel Soviet leaders that the Allied action in the White Sea "was not aimed against the Soviet Government": whereas a few days later, when they met the Soviet leaders again, Kemp and he had been told of "high-handed action by the Allied naval authorities on the western shores of the White Sea, including the shooting of three members of the Kem Soviet", a report which was subsequently confirmed. Young asserted that the local Soviet authorities had been ready to come to an agreement (which he had been negotiating) on the basis of an exchange of goods: but that any possibility of reaching a modus vivendi had been "swept away like a house of cards" by the Allied landing.

The landing had not proved a success: "We may thank God that there were no Germans there, if the Soviet troops alone have thrown us back upon Archangel". All it had done had been to cut off 150,000 of the 150 millions of Russia, and to make their lot a little easier, "on condition that they do exactly what we wish". Young invited the Allies to negotiate, and "to fit our actions towards Russia to the 'acid test' enunciated by President Wilson."

The publication of this letter had a more definite echo in the British press than the article in the Herald. The *Star*, the same day, quoted it at length, under the headings: "Allied Blunders in Russia. British Consul's Light on Situation. 'High handed action' ". The *Daily News* (December 23) published on its front page a detailed reply to the long apologia for intervention which Lord Milner, Secretary for War, had issued to the press on December 18: the wording of the article was clearly that of Young; and this was underlined by its demand, "where is Mr. Young's report from Archangel?"

By December 28, when Kemp's reply to Young was printed, the Foreign Office had begun to discuss what should be done. On December 19 Lord Curzon minuted: "Mr Young is a capable official who has done good work at Archangel and elsewhere, and is of course entitled to hold whatever opinions he may please. In fact, there is a great deal in this letter which merits serious consideration. But I submit that the proper channel through which Mr. Young should put forward his reflections is the Foreign Office, and I further submit that it is entirely subversive of all discipline, and contrary to the whole practice and traditions of the Government service, for an official still employed under the Secretary of State to ventilate his opinions in this manner. The growing attacks of British Bolsheviks and the *Westminster Gazette* upon our action in Russia may make it a little difficult to deal with Mr. Young as he should be dealt with, but it seems to me very difficult to allow an official who has behaved as Mr. Young has done to remain in the public service." Lord Hardinge echoed these sentiments: "I think Mr. Douglas Young must be told that his action in writing to the Press on political matters without previous consultation with the Foreign Office is inconsistent with the rules governing the public service".[127]

It may be of course that these officials were not aware at the time that Young had tried to do precisely what they wanted — to "put forward his objections to the Foreign Office" — and that he had almost in so many words been refused permission to do so.

In his reply to Young, Admiral Kemp adopted a tone, as Young said in his further letter, "more appropriate to the quarterdeck or schoolroom". He called Young's letter "mischievous, tending to discourage a national enterprise, a mass of false suggestions and innuendo and of obscure references to concrete events". In particular, he claimed that he did not know of the Allies' intention to occupy Archangel when he spoke to the Soviet there, and that his assurance had referred only to the Murman coast: and that he had moreover given a warning to them that "any orders received from the Allied Governments would be carried into effect by their forces". As regards the disarming of Red Guards at Kem, this had been "mutually agreed", and the three members of the Soviet there had been shot while "offering armed resistance". Young, he admitted, was right about the date of Cromie's death, but his own assertions about illtreatment of Allied subjects were true. The Soviet Government had been showing an "ever-growing pro-German policy", while the British Government "had been conciliatory to the last degree" — and he knew of no cases of the British Government playing "a double game". The Bolshevik elements at Archangel were "cowardly bandits" who had fled with many millions of roubles stolen from public and private funds. Russia was starving, not because of the occupation of Archangel, but because a "tyranny and anarchy had closed the avenues of transport and sources of supply". The Soviet Government had repeatedly proclaimed itself "the champion of anarchy and of the extermination of the upper classes".

Finally, Kemp declared that the only relationship which could exist between the Soviet leaders and the British Government was that "of criminal and judge" — and added to his previous programme for the Allies in Russia, "the control for a time of all means of transport and communication, and of the economic system in Russia generally".

127. F.O. 371, vol. 3350.

The reader will be able to judge from the documents surveyed earlier, giving a more intimate picture of the aims, methods and preparation of intervention all round the borders of Russia and in her interior, how far Kemp's assertions corresponded with the facts. Douglas Young could not have been aware of many of them. But he knew the essentials: and on these he based his further reply, printed by *The Times* on January 6, 1919.

Young pointed out that on the one point of the safety of British subjects, which was "a matter peculiarly calculated to appeal to public sentiment" on the eve of an election, Kemp had admitted he was wrong in stating that they had been maltreated before the Allied descent upon Archangel. Kemp's statement at Archangel itself on July 6 about the aims of intervention, whatever he considered they meant, had conveyed the meaning which Young suggested in his first letter — and this had been proved because "the Soviet authorities immediately responded by allowing the Allied refugees to proceed". British residents at Archangel, "so far from being at any time molested", had been given many privileges — and "if they could speak their minds", they would complain not of the Bolsheviks but of the fleeing Allied diplomatic representatives. Kemp would probably recall having told the Archangel Soviet leaders between July 6 and 11 that he personally thought the British Government should have recognised the Soviet Government. Without wishing to follow Kemp in all his other "absurdities" and distortions, it was a fact that "the menace from Murmansk closed the Soviet ranks at Archangel and throughout Russia". Answering Kemp's accusations about the resistance at Archangel, Young said the Russians were not a nation of cowards, and that their momentary panic was "due to the unexpected bombing by Allied planes against which they had no defence" and to their organisation being filled with Russian officers in the upper grades who intended from the first to betray them. Within a week of the landing they had held up the Allied advance, and still held it up. The Soviet authorities could hardly have been expected to leave Treasury and bank funds "for our convenience", whereas the Cossack officers who had arrested the Consuls had "appropriated and divided among themselves several million roubles of public money".

It was not yet the time, Young ended, to expose "the whole sordid story" of the activities of British representatives which could not be tolerated by the Soviet Government: but it would come, and he warned against "misrepresentation and suppression of facts" which could only aggravate a difficult and dangerous situation.

On the subject of the treatment of British subjects at Archangel (it may be noted in parenthesis) Young wrote many years later: "The word of the British Consul in this respect was almost law. A Consular certificate secured to a British subject immediate and complete immunity from billetting in his house". Local officials did their best with feeding and housing large numbers of British and Allied subjects coming from the interior.

Whether or not the Admiral attempted a third letter is not known: the newspaper printed no further correspondence from either side. It is not hazarding an improbable guess that Kemp received official advice to cease his attacks. For later, on April 8, 1919, Sir Ronald Graham (Acting Permanent Under-Secretary of State) in discussion with Young about his action in writing to *The Times*, suggested that perhaps sanction for Kemp's original reply to Young's letter of December 19 "had previously been obtained from His Majesty's Government" (Young's record of the conversation).

The correspondence certainly caused a great sensation, particularly in the working class, and greatly helped the "Hands Off Russia!" movement which had already begun. The Liberal newspapers already mentioned also intensified their attacks on the Government's Russian policy, as even a cursory reference to their leading articles would show. At the end of February, 1919, the exchange of letters was reprinted as a pamphlet by the People's Russian Information Bureau (set up the previous autumn by various Socialist organisations). The pamphlet was entitled: "British Consul Replies to Anti-Bolshevik Slanders" and had a very wide sale (as the present writer, demobilised from the British army a few days after Young's final reply appeared, can testify). Young's own copy bears the note in his handwriting: "This pamphlet was issued without any reference to me. D.Y."

In the Foreign Office, the reaction was quite violent, although restrained by an obvious fear of the growing public opposition to invervention.

Already on December 31, 1918, before Young's final reply appeared, one high official (Sir Victor Wellesley) minuted: "Mr Young merits at least a severe reprimand, and personally I think he should be dismissed, but I cannot of course say whether this course would be politic in present circumstances". This was endorsed by Mr. J.D. Gregory and Sir George Clerk. Someone else added: "I certainly think he ought to be dismissed, if there are no political objections to that course". Lord Curzon suggested: "We could deal with *The Times* correspondence by asking for an explanation, but the *Herald* article is outrageous. On the other hand, Mr. Young is very possibly riding for a fall, and may at this moment acquire cheap popularity. Perhaps we might begin by instructing him to proceed, if his leave is over, to another post (out of Russia) and see what he will do". The

Chief Clerk wrote: "This seems to me an outrageous case, and if any discipline is to be maintained in the service it should be treated drastically. I think that Mr. Young should be asked to furnish explanations, and be informed that, pending the receipt of satisfactory explanations from him, he is suspended from service." [128]

The appearance of Young's second letter clinched the matter, and on January 25, 1919, Lord Curzon (acting head of the Foreign Office in Mr. Balfour's absence) directed that a letter be sent to him referring to the article and the two letters. These contained "criticisms of the policy of His Majesty's Government with regard to the situation in Russia, and to the conduct of British officials to whom the carrying out of that policy was entrusted". Officials employed by His Majesty's Government (as Young could hardly fail to be aware) were not permitted to publish in the public press "any views they may hold, or opinions they may have formed, in the course of their duties in carrying out their instructions". Accordingly the letter instructed Young to furnish explanations of his conduct, and informed him that pending receipt of satisfactory explanations he was suspended from the exercise of his functions as an officer of the Consular service.

It was significant of the embarrassment felt by Young's superiors that, in the original draft prepared by Wellesley, the following sentence occurrred: "I am to point out to you that you would have been entitled at any time to forward to this Department the expression of your views and opinions relative to the policy of H.M.G. in Russia, which would have received the careful consideration of the Secretary of State". But it was struck out, for reasons which will be clear to the reader of what Young wrote about his interview at the Foreign Office on his return from Archangel, when he was told in effect *not* to write such an "expression of views and opinions".

Moreover he had not been exercising any consular functions since the end of October, 1918: and, when pointing this out in the reply to the Foreign Office (January 28, 1919), Young asked whether he was to suspend his work at the Department of Overseas Trade. This brought a further outburst of indignant remarks at the Foreign Office: "Mr. Young is vainly trying to wriggle out of it" (J.D.G.): "This is a mere quibble" (H.E.S.): "Suspension surely means stoppage of pay and cessation of exercise of official duties" (Chief Clerk): "Of course" (V.W.).[129] A letter from Lord Curzon's private secretary so notified him on February 7, 1919.

At this very moment (he wrote three years later), "I found myself

---

128. F.O. 371. vol. 3350. pp. 370-371.

129. F.O. 369. vol. 1213. paper 16013.

faced with a difficult private situation. My wife received news of the death of her mother in Russia: and the effect of that news was increased by the realisation that the landed and other property which she would have inherited in the ordinary course was lost to her through revolutionary action. I accordingly seemed to be faced by the choice, in the matter of my trouble with the F.O., of going through with what I conceived to be my public duty, or submitting to force of circumstances" i.e. regaining the employment which was his livelihood. At this moment there appeared the "Prinkipo proposal" — the invitation by the Supreme Allied Council to all the warring groups in Russia to attend a peace conference on Prinkipo Island in the Sea of Marmora, near Istanbul — and this gave some hope, Young thought, of a speedy liquidation of the civil war and intervention, making further action on his part "superfluous". He therefore sent in his explanation on March 4, 1919.

During the interval, the Foreign Office took advantage of a further unexpected opportunity, unknown to Young for a time, to visit its displeasure upon him. On February 25 the Shipping Controller, Sir Joseph Maclay, had written to Mr. Balfour about "the exceptionally meritorious work done at Archangel during the early part of 1918 by Mr. Consul Young". From the time that the Naval Transport Staff was withdrawn on December 18, 1917, Young had taken charge of British interests and especially of shipping work. "Not only was Mr. Young's position difficult and dangerous owing to the disturbed political conditions, but a large part of the duties performed by him were, it is suggested, entirely outside the scope of ordinary Consular work, involving negotiations for the use of Russian tonnage, loading and discharging cargoes and other similar services, all of a purely shipping character. It was undoubtedly the means of saving a very considerable sum of money for His Majesty's Government". The letter asked Balfour to concur in asking the Treasury to pay Young a special gratuity of £200.[130]

The sum would have been of material help in Young's circumstances, as well as giving him encouragement. Doubtless for those very reasons the suggestion was far from welcome to the Foreign Office. "In ordinary circumstances the question of this payment would have been one for discussion: now it is out of the question", was the first comment (H.E. Satow) The second was more circumspect: "This proposal of the Ministry of Shipping is awkward, as of course no one doubts the value of Mr. Young's work. It seems to me only fair that we should wait till he has answered, so that if his explanation can as I hope be accepted we can concur in the Ministry

130. F.O. 369, vol. 1213, paper 31457.

of Shipping's proposal" (Sir G. Clerk). In keeping with this suggestion, the reply to Sir Joseph Maclay asked him please to defer actions in the matter for the moment.[131]

On March 4, 1919, Young sent in his explanation which is in his personal papers. Its essence had already been told in the foregoing pages. But the following key points seem worth emphasising. He had wished to correct Kemp's inaccuracies, published with "the avowed object of influencing public opinion". The British Government had made a "fundamental error" in assuming that the anti-war policy of the Soviet Government, "dictated primarily by economic exhaustion", was ipso facto pro-German. The Soviet Government, being anxious to find an agreement on economic cooperation with the Allies, had been willing to tolerate British activities against the enemy in North Russia, "provided this was not done over their heads and without their sanction". But "irresponsible agents of the British Military Command" were allowed to enter into dishonourable and dangerous intrigues with the anti-Soviet factions, "with or without the consent of His Majesty's Government". This activity (of which the Soviet authorities were aware), coupled with the risings of the Czecho-slovaks and at Yaroslavl, destroyed Soviet confidence in the word and good faith of the Allies. He himself, despite his series of telegrams in June and July, 1918, had been given no clear guidance or information about British policy. He was surprised to be told on his return to England, that he should not submit a report to the Foreign Office, although by this time, "the failure of the Archangel expedition was self-evident". The Government, he now realised, were evidently determined not to hear anything "not to the discredit of the Soviet Government" — and this impression was strengthened by the campaign in the press, using "unreliable and one-sided evidence" to prepare the public for military intervention on a large scale — when in fact "a peaceful understanding with the Soviet Government could have been reached". Considering that the British Government had employed "methods which were not in accord with true and honest dealing", he had wished to awaken public opinion to the real meaning of a war with Russia. He knew that his action was "a technical breach of discipline", involving possible loss of his liveli-hood: because he "placed truth before tradition, and human life above merely official considerations", he had decided to take it. Young added that other persons receiving pay from public funds had published articles, letters, speeches and lectures on the Russian situation, based on their experience as officials in that country — and his offence seemed to be, not the act of publicity, but in his happening to differ from the views of the Foreign Office. He claimed

131. After the acceptance of Young's apology, Curzon agreed to the payment (May 10).

moreover that the policy he advocated had in fact been subsequently adopted by the Peace Conference.

Young's obvious misfortune was that he did not know of the considered Cabinet decisions of December 21, 1917, and that consequently he did not understand that British actions in respect of Archangel were only part of a whole network of activities of which the competent British authorities, political and diplomatic no less than military, were fully aware and which they encouraged. To reproach them, therefore, with using methods at Archangel in regard to Soviet Russia which were "not in accord with truth and honest dealing" was irrelevant when writing to one of the principal departments involved from the very first in those methods (as the reader has seen, but as Young did not know).

The comments of its responsible officials took the form which could be expected in these circumstances — though still tempered by anxiety about what increasingly restive public opinion would say.

"The only excuse he offers is that he alleges he was told that no report from him was required. . . Personally I should be sorry if it were decided to dispense with Mr. Young's services, as he is extremely able" (E.F. Gye, head of the Consular Department, March 8). "It would evidently be useless to reason with him... The only point that occurs to me is whether he would not be rather dangerous if dismissed from the service. He can make out rather a plausible pro-Bolshevist case as regards Archangel, and it would be extremely inconvenient to have him at large, countering such anti-Bolshevist propaganda as we are able to conduct". He might be "muzzled" by letting him stay, on an undertaking "not to misbehave any more" (J.D. Gregory, April 3). Sir George Clerk, (April 3) confirmed that Young came to see him, but asserted that he had particularly asked Young to report on the situation "when he was fit enough". "I knew that his views, though not those of our own local military authorities, would be those of an intelligent man who looked at things from another angle". Nevertheless, there had been "a gross and deliberate breach of duty, knowingly committed", and leniency "should not go further than allowing him to resign". Sir Ronald Graham (April 4) thought that Young "certainly writes a good letter", though his arguments were beside the point. However, "I am a good deal impressed by the general testimony to his ability": and Sir Ronald suggested a reprimand. Lord Curzon (the same day) said: "The unfortunate thing is that in substance he has been proved right". Young's personal attack was on General Poole — "and it seems now to be generally admitted that that officer made a deplorable mess of it". He agreed that Graham should see Young and get an apology from him.[132]

132. F.O. 369, vol. 1213, paper 36519.

At no point, of course, did any comment by these officials suggest that anything was wrong in the general policy of the British Government towards Russia — really the essential point of Young's letter of explanation.

On April 5, 1918, he received a letter inviting him to come and see Sir Ronald Graham, and the interview took place on April 8. In his unpublished account, Young wrote: "Sir Ronald Graham was very friendly, but seemed ill at ease. After referring in most flattering terms to my services at Archangel and to my previous record, he hinted that I might save my job by making a formal statement of regret, not for my opinions (he expressly stated that), but for the technical offence of having expressed them publicly without the permission of the Secretary of State. No reference was made by him to the circumstances which led to my action, the matter being treated solely as one of discipline". After thinking it over, and in view of the fact that the Prinkipo proposals had been made — even though the Foreign Office officials seemed determined to ignore what he considered to be the substance of the question — Young on April 10 sent a letter of apology for his "serious offence against service discipline". Nearly three weeks passed before he received an acknowledgement from Lord Curzon — "very different in tone from the conciliatory conversation of the Under-Secretary", and threatening him with "dismissal from His Majesty's service" if there were any repetition of this grave offence (April 30, 1919). A few days later Young was paid the £200 due to him from the Ministry of Shipping.

A new clash between Young's principles and Foreign Office practices arose almost immediately, however. On May 5, 1919, the Foreign Office notified the Treasury that Young was being sent as Vice-Consul to Novorossiisk, "where his services are urgently needed" and on May 9 it wrote to Young that, before proceeding there, he should work for a short time at the Russian and Scandinavian section of the Department of Overseas Trade, "in order that you may become acquainted with recent trade developments in the Black Sea regions".

That region, as everyone knew, was one in which Allied support of General Denikin was in full swing, following his (and the other White leaders') rejection of the Prinkipo proposals. Consequently the "offer" meant — as the Foreign Office understood just as well as Young himself — sending him back "to cooperate in a movement which I regard not merely as a lost but also as an immoral cause". In view of the position in which he had been placed at Archangel, he wrote in a later memorandum, it was a movement in which "I could not take part with any honour". Perhaps that was the very reason why the offer had been made to him.

Young therefore decided to decline. He was already suffering from considerable nervous overstrain, and the work at Novorossiisk would undoubtedly have added to it. So, to avoid any further controversy, he asked (May 15) to be allowed to remain unemployed without salary, for a period of six months, " in order that I may enjoy for that further period complete rest and freedom from official responsibilities of any kind". This was in fact a quixotic gesture: under Foreign Office regulations he would have been entitled to half-pay.

But, instead of responding in kind, Lord Curzon gave an unmistakable demonstration of that petty spitefulness towards those whom he regarded as his inferiors for which he was famous. A letter sent to Young on June 10 — it had taken nearly four weeks to concoct — informed him, on behalf of Curzon, not only that he was granted six months' leave without pay, but also that "the period without pay cannot be allowed to count for increase of ultimate pension".

From that time, Young was not only without emoluments of any kind, but also earning no pension rights. He was in effect in the position of a private British citizen, not committing any official institution — least of all the Foreign Office — by any lawful action he might take. In fact, he scrupulously avoided any public activity whatsoever.

However, in the course of that summer, the Allied plans for their forces in North Russia to join up with Kolchak's anticipated advance from the East had utterly failed. Not only were their forces, as previously mentioned, held up at a relatively short distance from Archangel, but the Russian military units which had been formed under their protection had mutinied on several occasions, killing their British officers: while American units had also shown unmistakable signs of discontent. Kolchak, on the other hand, had been heavily defeated by the Red Army, and his forces were in full retreat. Moreover, it became clear that certain new battalions who had been sent out to Archangel in May, on the pretext of covering the evacuation of existing forces, were in reality intended merely as reinforcements, without any real preparation for withdrawal. On the contrary, the campaign was to continue throughout the coming winter of 1919-20. The "Hands Off Russia!" movement in Britain correspondingly became more intense, particularly after the Labour Party Conference at the end of June had adopted a resolution calling for joint action with the TUC to put an end to intervention "by the unreserved use of their political and industrial power".[133]

133. W.P. and Z. Coates, *A History of Anglo-Soviet Relations,* (London, 1943) pp. 141-145.

At this juncture, relying on the fact that (as he thought) he was in the position of a private citizen, Douglas Young took advantage of what he conceived to be the privilege of a private citizen, and on August 6, 1919, wrote to Prime Minister Lloyd George. He recalled his warnings to the Foreign Office, cabled to them in June and July, 1918, while "in sole charge of British interests as H.M. Consul at Archangel", and that he had been proved right. He proceeded: "The position of the Allied forces in Archangel appears to be causing His Majesty's Government great anxiety. I am convinced that the Soviet Government of Russia has no desire to inflict upon the Allied forces at Archangel anything in the nature of a military disaster, but would be satisfied with the moral victory which our peaceful withdrawal would give them. Such withdrawal has in any case been decided upon by His Majesty's Government in words, and there is consequently no reason why it should not be carried out without the loss of a single soldier. Aggressive action on our part, however, such as the sending of more generals and troops, or the unsuccessful attempt to reoccupy Onega as reported in today's press, under circumstances of appalling bloodshed and destruction, will only act as provocation, and may cause the Bolshevik command to lose all restraint, and to do that which is contrary both to their interests and ours".

For more than a year, Young went on, "I have suffered the usual lot of a minority of one, having been ignored by my Department as a rather dangerous lunatic, and regarded by my colleagues of the navy, army and diplomatic service as 'a good fellow with a bad kink' ". However, he was prepared to endeavour even now to secure the bloodless withdrawal which he still thought possible, taking his chance of getting through by Archangel to Vologda or Moscow at any personal risk. He was ready to take this risk, "not so much on behalf of a Government whose blindness and folly have so largely contributed to the present result, as in the interests of my country and humanity and gereral peace". British generals and admirals had hitherto conspicuously failed in Russia, he concluded, not because they were bad in their profession, but because they "know nothing and care less about the psychology of an alien race". Young appended a copy of his letter to the Foreign Office of March 4.

It may be noted that in fact W.H. Buckler, an attaché of the US Embassy in London, had reported earlier in the year, after a visit to Litvinov in Stockholm, that in the words of the Soviet representative, "unquestionably the Bolsheviki would agree to an armistice on the Archangel front at any time".[134]

The concluding passages in Young's letter could hardly be regarded as tactful in the circumstances; but they were far milder

134. W.P. & Z. Coates, *Armed Intervention in Russia.* (London 1935) pp. 162-163.

than the language then commonly in use by the opponents of intervention.

However, in all probability what decided the fate of Young's letter was neither the possibility of an armistice in the North nor the tone of his references to the Lloyd George Coalition Government. It was what in those months seemed the biggest event in the Civil War as yet — the White Armies' victories in South Russia and the Ukraine in June, July and August. Bloodshed in the Archangel region was a mere drop in the ocean, compared with the prospects which those victories seemed to open.

At all events, what Lloyd George did was to send Young a formal acknowledgement — and to forward his letter without comment to Lord Curzon. This immediately reopened the floodgates of doubt and denunciation at the Foreign Office.

"No good purpose would be served by Mr. Young proceeding to Archangel", wrote Major-General Thwaites, Director of Military Intelligence, to whom the matter had evidently been referred for his opinion (September 1, 1919). "It is irregular for a Consul to approach the Prime Minister directly, without reference to the Secretary of State, on general questions of policy and in regard to an appointment for himself. Such conduct would as a rule bring upon a Consul a severe and deserved snub. It is however clear from Mr. Young's previous doings (a) that he is a valuable public servant and (b) that he is the kind of person who will never be constrained by snubs or remonstrances or reprimands to observe the rules of conduct and discipline. As he is admittedly an able man, it is probably best for the public service to put up with his crankiness, unless and until it is deemed necessary to get rid of him" (Mr O'Malley). He suggested that no reply be sent. Mr. J.C. Tilley wrote: "I do not think we can dismiss him for writing to the Prime Minister to offer his services, although the tone of his letter is most impertinent".

Others were more determined. J.D. Gregory wrote (September 8) "Mr. Young is incorrigible. He has no sense of propriety whatsoever. It is clearly not so bad to go to the Prime Minister as to the Press behind the back of one's Department. But it shows that he does not know what discipline means" And he concluded: "Leniency would be demoralising".

Obviously the officials were worried lest Young should take his stand on the obvious position that to deny a citizen the right to address the head of the Government privately, on a matter of national importance, and without in any way questioning the policy of the branch of the Civil Service for which he was working, was a serious matter. Moreover, he had made a suggestion which obviously would involve considerable peril for himself without any question of "appointment" or reward. But they knew that the question of departmental discipline — even though that discipline was not in fact infringed or involved, since Young was in effect out of the service for the time being — would be a very convenient ground on which Lord Curzon could take action against a man who in effect was questioning the policy of war on the Bolsheviks, a policy to which Curzon was passionately devoted.

So it proved. Curzon's comment was: "I have had enough of Mr. Young, and do not propose to reemploy him". It is relevant to recall that at this moment Denikin's army had reached Orel, barely 200 miles from Moscow, and the general belief expressed by the newspapers and in the Government parties was that the fall of the Soviet capital would follow in a few days.

On October 9, therefore, Lord Curzon had a letter sent to Young, recalling Young's expression of regret for communicating with the press, and continuing that nevertheless he had now

> "not only been guilty of a further breach of discipline in having, while in the service of the Foreign Office, communicated direct with the Prime Minister without reference to the Secretary of State, but you have in your letter to Mr. Lloyd George given expression to further criticism of the policy of His Majesty's Government, and have referred with approval to criticisms already made.
>
> "If you were a private individual you would, so far as the Secretary of State is concerned, be at liberty to hold and to ventilate, either in the press or otherwise, such views as you might see fit to advocate. But this was not your position, and so long as you occupy a post in the public service you are bound by the same rules of discipline as apply to other public servants. From what has occurred it is clear to the Secretary of State that, holding the opinions you do, you will find it as difficult in the future as you have found it in the past to be bound by such rules, or, if your views do not commend themselves to your superiors, to abide by their decision.
>
> "In these circumstances, it will not be possible to find for you further employment in the Consular Service, your connection with which must be held to have come to an end".

At no point in this characteristically pompous letter did Lord Curzon mention what rule prevented a "public servant" communicating privately to the Prime Minister of his country on a matter, not internal to the Foreign Office, but of national policy. Nor did he attemtp to justify the logic of comparing such an action with the

135. F.O. 369, vol. 1213, Young's letter of August 6, 1919, and covering comments, September 1-9, 1919.

articles in, or letters to, the press.

Thus at a stroke Young was deprived both of his career and even of pension rights already earned. Some time later, he seems to have seriously considered taking up the matter "before the several organs of appeal which lie open to a permanent official of the Civil Service dismissed by administrative action". Stating this in a letter to the Foreign Office on April 29, 1920, he formally enquired whether Curzon's decision was to be regarded as final. To this Curzon replied in the affirmative on May 8, 1920. But although the collapse of the White armies was now complete, the large-scale Polish invasion of Soviet Russia had begun only a few days before (April 25, 1920). The King himself had on May 7 sent a telegram of congratulation to the Polish leader, Marshal Pilsudsky, ostensibly on the anniversary of the Polish Constitution of 1791 but, as was universally understood, really on the success of his invasion; and for the moment the forces of war in the British Cabinet were obviously in the ascendant. Perhaps it was for this reason that Young appears to have taken no action of the kind he mentioned in April: but he left no positive indication explaining his decision.

It should be mentioned, in any case, that at the time there did not exist in Great Britain the powerful trade unions and other associations of civil servants which grew up many years later, and on whom Young in other conditions could have relied for support.

From a lengthy restatement of his care which he addressed to the Foreign Office on August 24, 1921, however, (when de facto relations had been established with Soviet Russia), there can be no doubt that Young throughout, with his upbringing and his profound conviction of the traditional uprightness of British public men and British officials, was restrained by the hope of ultimately persuading Lord Curzon to reconsider the case in all aspects. He even urged in this letter that he had "refused invitations to speak on public platforms and declined inducements to publish the story as I know it", as evidence of the good faith in which he had acted. But this conciliatory attitude brought no response whatsoever, except for a curt letter from the Foreign Office stating that Lord Curzon "declines to reopen the question of your employment or to continue the correspondence".

Appendix to Chapter 13

The mutinies and desertions among the Russian troops raised under the supervision and with the material aid of the British military authorities at Archangel may be detailed here, in continuation of the references in the letters received by Douglas Young.

It is only fair to say that the archives of those authorities mention, especially at first, many individual desertions—chiefly by night—from the Soviet forces during the occupation. But the Soviet troops were for many months of 1918 and even at the beginning of 1919 only at a very early stage of organisation as a cohesive army. In the Archangel province there were among them some fairly well-trained and equipped, and above all politically determined units of industrial workers, sailors and Bolshevik soldiers. But the majority, both volunteers and mobilised, were armed villagers, enlisted hastily at many places scattered among the vast forests of the region, who were not by any means all supporters of the Bolsheviks at first. Moreover, among their Soviet commanders there were some officers whose sympathies were with the other side, and who acted accordingly (as the records show).

On the other hand, those raising the armed forces at Archangel had the advantage of offering better food, clothing and equipment, and for the most part of being themselves, both British and Russian, experienced officers and NCOs: in the Slavo-British Legion, indeed, 50% of them were by regulation British. Mutinies among the troops under Allied control were therefore more politically significant than the individual desertions from the camp of their adversaries.

The following table gives a more comprehensive picture (though not necessarily complete) than do the few references in the letters from Wiskemann—or for that matter than do histories of the period published up to now.

No.	*Date*	*Unit*	*Action taken*	*Reference*
1.	29 August 1918	Slavo-British Allied Legion.	"A section fired on its officers and deserted"	WO.95.5419
2.	29 October 1918	Conscripts at Alexander Nevski Barracks	"Refused to go on parade Reasons (i) officers still wearing (?Tsarist) stars (ii) They would not fight for the English King (iii) They would not salute (iv) Wanted larger rations".	*ibid.*

3.	3 December 1918	1st Archangel Regt.	"Mutinied" (disarmed, 13 ringleaders shot)	*ibid. and* WO.33.950
4.	30 December 1918	2nd company of 1st Archangel Regt.	Attack "held up owing to refusal to advance" (at *Tarasevo).*	WO.95.5419
5.	21 January 1919	"Mobilised Russn. battalion"	"Proved useless, one coy. actually refusing to attack" *(Shenkursk)*	*ibid.*
6.	25 April 1919	2nd battn. 3rd North Russian Regt.	"9 Russian officers killed". total 300 men missing. Enemy during night admitted to *Tulgas,* surrounded HQ. billet. *(Tulgas).*	*ibid.*
7.	27 April 1919	Machinegun coy. Russn. Shenkursk battn.	Killed 2 officers, scattered, some to Red Army. Numbers involved believed 150.	WO.33.966
8.	14 May 1919	1st coy. 8th North Russian Regt.	Refused to embark to go up river. "2 officers were killed. I regret to report that I had to shoot 15, but the companies are back at duty". 2nd coy. disarmed. *(Pinega).*	*ibid. also* WO.95 (appendices)
9	7 July 1919	3rd coy, 1st battn. Slavo-British Legn. also machine-gun coy. 4th N.Russn. Regt.	"Determined mutiny, 2am". 4 British, 4 Russn. offrs. killed, 2 Brit. 2 Russn. offrs. wounded. 200 escaped to Bolsheviks. Suppressed by gunfire of river flotilla. 11 shot, rest given prison terms. Battn. disarmed, made into a Labour battn. 2nd battn. Slavo-British Legn. also *(Topsa-Troitsa* area).	WO.33.910 WO.33.967A WO.95.5419
10.	21 July 1919	5th N.Russn.Regt.	"Mutinied 1a.m." 3,000 infantry, 1,000 other arms, including four 75s, "gone over to the Bolsheviks". Whole Onega front in Red Army hands. *(Chikuyevo).*	*as above*
11.	22 July 1919	12 men of 3rd coy. 6th N.Russn.Regt.	Deserted to Bolsheviks. 2nd. coy. same Regt. was disarmed and 4 shot.	WO.95.5419
12.	3 August 1919	Russn. troops on *SS.Wharton Belle,* just arrived from Onega.	British sailor killed. Mutineers transferred to HMS *Fox. (Archangel).*	*ibid.*
13.	24 August 1919	1 sergt. and 10 men of 1st.N.Russn. Regt.	Deserted to Red Army with rifles.	*ibid.*

14.	24 August 1919	20 men of 1st. North Russn. Regt.	"Disaffection among them" *Monitor 26* sent there, and mutineers brought to Archangel *(Krasnaya Gorka)*	*ibid.*
15.	26 August 1919	Russn.C.O., 4th North Russn.Regt. states: men say when British go they will murder officers and go home.	*(Dvina front)*	*ibid.*
16.	27 August 1919	3rd.coy, (4th ?) N. Russn.Regt.	Refused to parade when ordered. *(Dvina front)*	*ibid.*
17.	28 August 1919	16 men of 8th coy. 4th North Russn. Rgt.	Deserted with rifles *(Vaga)*	*ibid.*
18.	29 August 1919	"Large desertions of Russian troops with and without arms".	1st,2nd,3rd,5th coys. of 4th N.Russn.Regt. disarmed	*ibid.*

Two volumes, published at Archangel in 1967 — one of reminiscences of 1918-1919 *(V Boiakh za Sovietski Sever),* the other a collection of documents of the period *(Borba za Torzhestvo Sovietskoi Vlasti na Severe)* — describe several of these mutinies from the Soviet side.

By July, 22 1919, General Ironside (commanding all Allied forces in North Russia) was already cabling to the War Office that "the state of the Russian troops is such that it is certain my efforts to consolidate a Russian National Army are definitely a failure. As early evacuation as possible is essential now unless the British force here is to be increased" (WO.33.967A). A memorandum drawn up by the Chief of the Imperial General Staff, on the basis of such reports as those quoted, stated accordingly that "the situation at Archangel had radically changed... We had failed to create a reliable Russian Army... Now there was nothing to be gained by British forces remaining at Archangel a day longer than necessary" (WO.33.950).

Thus Douglas Young's condemnation of the Archangel invasion was overwhelmingly justified by events within barely twelve months.

PART V

14

Young now found himself in a situation which he had never before experienced. Not only had his livelihood (£800 a year, with allowances) and his prospects of a pension disappeared, but he felt an added moral responsibility to his Russian wife, her father and their Russian maid (he had brought both to England in 1918). His mother-in-law had recently died, and the landed property which this would have brought Mrs. Young before the revolution was substantial, while Young had lost his savings in Russian bonds. What savings he had in British banks began to dwindle rapidly, and he had, much against his will, to accept generous help from his father.

He did what he could to earn a living in these new circumstances, writing articles and short stories of Russian life, lecturing, doing some work for the Red Cross, and even breeding dogs and keeping chickens at his small house in the country. But some of the difficulties he encountered can be illustrated from exchanges with the editor of the League of Nations Union journal, who in October, 1919, asked Young for an article on the possible admission of Russia to the League and on the attitude which should be adopted towards the White leaders Kolchak and Denikin if they did not succeed in overthrowing the Soviet Government, or alternatively if they did. Young responded with an article explaining why the League of Nations should do the opposite of what the Allies had been doing to Russia for fifteen months. The editor acknowledged receipt, but later decided not to use it. He had seen Colonel John Ward — formerly trade union organiser of labourers before the war — about it, and had decided that he could not take responsibility for an article recommending Young's line of policy, except as material for the next League of Nations Union handbook. Young expostulated with him, pointing out that Col. Ward was with a British military force in Siberia, hand in glove with Admiral Kolchak and obviously no adequate judge. He (Young) was quite willing for his article to appear over his own name, if need be. But the editor refused.

This incident fully reflects the prevailing atmosphere of 1919 where Russian affairs were concerned. In general, whenever there arose any prospects of employment, or even of placing an article in a publication of general interest, they disappeared directly Young's Foreign

Office record became known. But never for a moment did he relax his campaign against intervention, and against its anti-Soviet heritage in the years after intervention ended.

As late as May, 1922, incidentally, he was still hoping that there was a chance of election to a fellowship at one of the Universities — despite the fact that Lord Curzon himself was one of the board of electors! Of course, nothing came of it: the Foreign Office's hostility to Young continued. One characteristic instance has survived in his papers. The "New Leader" (organ of the Independent Labour Party) at the end of December, 1923, published an article by him on Russo-British trade which was replying to an allegation in the "Times Trade Supplement" that the obstacle was not absence of diplomatic recognition, as the Labour movement was insisting, but the State monopoly of foreign trade in the USSR. Young, after showing the possibilities, pointed out that it was the "ill-considered intervention" by the Allies which had enhanced difficulties caused by the revolution, and had completely destroyed Russia's capacity to buy for the time being. He urged the Government to end "the official quarrel with the Soviet Government". Appended to the copy of the article in the Foreign Office files was the comment that, though Young's statements were "not incorrect", yet his "very incomplete and partial view of the position" were well known to the Department.

What sustained Young's morale in these painful years was the continued evidence that he had been right in his judgment of events at Archangel, together with the signs of approval which came from many intelligent people at home. Thus, Wiskemann wrote to him (December 10, 1918): "I will not say much re local affairs. Someone at home seems to object to my ideas (or rather our ideas) on the subject, which are *protivopolojennye* (opposed) to those of H.M.G., unfortunately. Your swan song is of course completely justified — but no one will pay any attention to it. Nauseating is just the word as regards the press at home". On December 14 Wiskemann added that there had been a mutiny among the Russian troops raised by the Allies — "as is of course inevitable" — and 13 had been shot. Even when the Allies, thanks to intensified supplies of arms, food and clothing, had succeeded in the spring in getting some sort of Russian army together, Wiskemann commented (May 7, 1919): "I have no doubt the whole thing would collapse like a pack of cards if we cleared out. The *Times* letters are praised by many, and anyway countenanced by most". Both Wiskemann and Cole were now trying to accept the *fait accompli*, which Young had refused to do, and were taking the line that "we must go on and see it through", now that there were still more Russian battalions: and there seemed to them

136. F.O. 371, vol. 3338, 2 January, 1924.

no doubt that before long the Allied forces would join up with Kolchak. But of course there was no such junction, while several of the new battalions shot their Russian and British officers and went over to the Red Army. By July 23, 1919, Wiskemann was writing that "the situation is anything but good, and God knows what may be the end of it". He foresaw the possibility of "my forced and sudden departure": meanwhile, the activities of the authorities were "a form of White terror". On August 14, Wiskemann wrote of the extraordinary currency, covered with Tsarist emblems, which he had described earlier: some of the emblems had been cut out by machine, but not all. Now "after working hard in the spring to get our beastly currency into circulation... we are working like hell to get it all *out* of circulation, and wind it up here any way". About ten people were working on this "very illegitimate child of the Treasury". And Cole's last letter to Young (August 17, 1919) admitted that "your worst fears concerning this enterprise have been realised". In fact, before long the Allied forces were making an undignified withdrawal from Archangel.

There is a striking document in the Foreign Office archives, from a different source, which illustrates very well the points made by Wiskemann, as well as those made by Young in his memorandum of the previous September. Although undated, it obviously refers to the situation fairly early in 1919. Written on note-paper of the Young Men's Christian Association, it says that the British "are not popular in this area" (Archangel), and gives the following indication of the reasons (a) "the overbearing and dominating attitude of the average British" (b) "we are not there as conquerors" (and ought to remember where England might have been, but for the Russian sacrifices of the first two years of the war) (c) "we must treat their womankind with the greatest respect and courtesy" (d) the Russians had tried to stamp out drunkenness: "shall we, by the example of our excesses, thrust her back to such endeavours?" (e) they should guard against the abuse of hospitality: "A Russian gentleman in Archangel asked me, 'why is it that the English officers I ask to dine with me offer to sell me whiskey and cigarettes at very high prices?' " (f) the men engaged in propaganda work were mostly "men with pre-war commercial experience": if they had no other outlook, they should not be employed (g) "We should altogether stop talking about Bolshevism."

The writer signed himself F. Komlosy. He was in fact the Revd. Francis Ference Komlosy, M.C., Chaplain to the Forces 1916-1918, and in the latter year Senior Chaplain to the 29th Division. His note was written, evidently, after a visit to Archangel. He was a former pupil of the present writer's school (Owen's School, Islington) and had been ordained in 1904, as the *Clerical Directory* for 1920 shows: that is, a clergyman of wide experience.

Next is a letter from Military Intelligence at Archangel to the Director of Military Intelligence in London, dated April 27, 1919. It suggested that leaflets signed by the British seamen's leader, Havelock Wilson, and similar officials would be "specially useful amongst workmen mobilised and fighting for the Bolsheviks".

The present generation may possibly know very little of the political features of Mr. Havelock Wilson; he was so far to the right of the trade union movement in Britain that he was frequently in conflict even with his most moderate colleagues leading other trade unions. The ludicrous suggestion was perhaps very eloquent of the political sagacity of the military, but undoubtedly would have dismayed anyone more familiar with the state of opinion in Britain among the mass of the people in 1919. This is clear from the observations made by Mr. Lindley, to whom evidently both documents had been submitted. He replied to Foreign Secretary Balfour (May 3, 1919): "The proper sphere for the military element is action: and by their action they can do far more good in the way of propaganda than any number of civilians by means of speeches and literature. So far as I know, there has been no brutality shown by our officers and men to the inhabitants: but it is notorious that there has been a great deal of drunkenness, and an organised exploitation of the population by a minority of both officers and men, who have sold to them at exorbitant prices stores imported by H.M.G. for the use of the forces or for the nourishment (of the region)". The General Officer Commanding had set his face against this practice unflinchingly. But Lindley feared that the other Allies had been "more scrupulous in their dealings with the people".[137]

However, what Young heard from Archangel was not a very great consolation for what he had gone through. More sustaining were the expressions of support which he received in Great Britain.

The following are extracts from some of the letters he received after the publication of his *Herald* article and his first letter to the *Times*. A Russian, D.A. Ruffman, F.R.G.S. (December 19, 1918) spoke of his "great interest and pleasure". He himself had suffered at the hands of the Bolsheviks, yet he was bound to recognise that the Allies had taken the wrong course in Russia. "There are other British officials here who have returned from Russia and who know, perhaps, more than you have written; but not one of them dares to write as you have done". On December 22, he had a letter from another Russian, J. Prelooker, author of popular books on Tsarist Russia, who said: "I have read with deep interest and sympathy your

137. F.O. 175, Box 12, contains both documents.

courageous and frank statements re the Allies' action in North Russia, and can only hope that at last the public may awaken to the real situation... and demand a new political course". D.M. Stevenson, active in the Labour movement, wrote from Glasgow (December 24) complimenting Young, and saying that "the conduct of our Government in Russia... if thoroughly understood, would be repudiated by the bulk of the nation". Another letter, in April, 1919, came from a young doctor, George H. Pearson, who while in Red Cross uniform had been arrested at Archangel in July, 1918, on suspicion of spying: "I think I shall always remember the quiet and sympathetic way in which you handled both myself and my 'captors' (who could not have treated me better than they did in the circumstances). I would also say that I heartily agree with your point of view".

Young had become, as mentioned earlier, a member of the "1917 Club", where he met a number of prominent Labour men, such as the I.L.P. leaders Philip Snowden and J. Ramsay Macdonald, Mr. C.R. Attlee, as well as more militant Socialists and democrats like Col. J. Wedgwood, Harold Laski, C.M. Joad, the actress Elsa Lanchester, H.G. Wells and others who learned with great sympathy of Young's history. At the end of August, 1920, when the Trades Union Congress and Labour Party had cooperated in using the threat of a general strike to force the Lloyd George government to abandon its threat of a new war with Russia, Young sent a copy of the memorandum on Archangel which he had prepared to R.L. Outhwaite, M.P., a well-known former Liberal who had gone over to Labour after the war. Outhwaite wrote: "I have read the manuscript with the greatest interest. It is a sordid and infamous business. If I might venture a criticism, I should have liked to have seen the counter-attack pressed further home". And shortly afterwards the eminent Liberal, professor Gilbert Murray, wrote (January 1, 1921) that Young's memorandum "seems to confirm some of one's worst suspicions. Your own position must have been extremely trying, indeed almost intolerable".

By 1923 Young was in close touch with E.D. Morel, the leading Labour Party specialist on foreign affairs and intransigent opponent of Allied policy towards Soviet Russia. On May 9 Young sent him a memorandum on intervention, of which a renewed threat had suddenly arisen through the notorious "Curzon ultimatum". When the Labour Party began seriously considering the basis of a settlement between Britain and the USSR, Young sent Morel another memorandum (December 27, 1923) on the question of a loan to the Soviet Government. He dealt notably with the Soviet counter-claims to be set off against the annulled Allied war credits to Tsarist Russia, recalling how the Russian army in 1914-15 had at an immense cost in lives and prisoners saved Paris and the Channel ports by its invasion of East Prussia. Two days later, answering some supplementary queries by Morel concerning the propaganda carried on by the Association of British Creditors of Russia, Young made the point that, in matters of financial probity, "the Bolsheviks are more to be trusted than their predecessors". He urged that the new Labour government should appoint "a committee of enquiry into the causes which led to the open breach with the Soviet Government in 1918" — in particular, that Macdonald should get hold of the Foreign Office Register Books, where all letters in and out were numbered and filed: fearing that otherwise incriminating documents would "disappear".

With the coming of the first Labour Government, in fact, Young was able to express himself in public with greater freedom, because of the obviously growing sympathy with his case for a reversal of the Conservative Government's policy of settled hostility to the Soviet Union, and for the establishment of normal diplomatic relations between the two countries. It must be recalled however that Macdonald was forced only by an open revolt of leading trade unionists and Labour M.Ps to carry out the pledges to this effect contained in the Labour Party's election manifesto of October, 1923, much earlier than he intended.

On February 18, 1924 Young wrote to the *Manchester Guardian* objecting to its dismissal of the Soviet counter-claim for destruction of property during the Allied invasion, and to its emphasis on compensation for properties confiscated *after* intervention began. That Liberal organ — hitherto opposing Tory policy towards the USSR — "merely acknowledged the letter", Young noted.

At the end of March, in Glasgow, Young gave two lectures on Russo-British relations at a Union of Democratic Control "School on Foreign Affairs", in which he exposed the economic and political causes of intervention and its consequences, with the need for a total reversal of policy. Many with whom the present writer has conversed remembered in after years his description of the attack on Archangel as "a third-rate naval imitation of the Jameson Raid". Of course at that time the deeply-laid plans for the "Raid", centring on Mr. Joseph Chamberlain, were as carefully buried in the archives as were the diplomatic and political preparations for intervention at Archangel.

Young had worked out a lantern lecture on the geography, people and folklore of Russia, with 70 slides. It was intended to be non-political: but its delivery often led to a highly political discussion of the same type as at the U.D.C. School—for example, at the London Busmen's Brotherhood at Westminster on 28 April, 1924.

In May a lecture on Finland developed into a pungent discusssion on the need for a turn to peaceful relations and trade with Soviet Russia. These are but some examples.

By this time an active movement for Young's reinstatement had begun.

On March 7, 1924, Langdon-Davies wrote to the new Labour Under-Secretary of State, Arthur Ponsonby, reminding him of the Young case, and how Young had taken "the unorthodox course of publishing what he regarded as the truth of what was happening in Russia", which the Foreign Office had suppressed. "He was supported by all of us in the Union of Democratic Control and general opposition camp at the time, but was of course turned out by the F.O.". Now that Labour was in power, these facts would be remembered. The reputation of the Labour movement was at stake, not only that of "so excellent and able a man as Douglas Young". Would Labour merely carry on "continuity of policy with those whom it has been busy condemning for years", or would it do justice to those who had honestly supported its principles, especially in the case of "such heroic actions as Young's?" At that time, "we all commended him, and said that he was the one just man". Now, with a knowledge of Russia "beyond question", he would be nothing but an asset to the Foreign Office.

Four days later, Ponsonby replied that "it is very wrong of me to have neglected Young's case", but he was going into it now. By March 17, he could add that he thought he had "successfully carried through the Douglas Young question", but formalities might "take a little time", and the further question of a post "must necessarily need arrangement". By March 31 Ponsonby had found that "the path turns out to be very rough": he had "caused a commotion" by getting a strong minute from MacDonald and then presenting it to the departments concerned. They were "cursing" him, not because of Young personally, but because "reinstatement is a rare and ticklish business". Ponsonby thought nevertheless that they would have to give in. Like most Labour MPs at the time, Ponsonby probably underestimated MacDonald's awe of the Foreign Office officials.

In fact, two months later nothing had happened. Margaret Wintringham, a Liberal M.P., had written early in May to Ponsonby about it, and had received an assurance (May 12) that the question was "now being dealt with". He personally had "a high opinion of his (Young's) abilities". Yet on June 6 he could only write to Young that he understood the latter's apprehensions at the delay, but that "reinstatement is a most difficult and complicated business". Even yet, Ponsonby could give him no definite news, "but the Prime Minister himself has had the matter before him", and Young therefore should not fear that his case had been "laid aside". This of course was a very non-committal document, and must have prepared Young, if not for refusal, at any rate for its very grudging outcome.

On July 2, 1924, at last, the Foreign Office by direction of Ramsay MacDonald wrote to Young that he might re-enter the Consular Service, but at a salary "not exceeding the amount of your substantive salary (excluding any acting allowance) at the time of your dismissal". What this meant, in plain language, was that Young, who was formally at Archangel only a Vice-Consul with local rank as Consul, would revert to his status as it was in 1915, at the beginning of his service at Archangel! Moreover, "in accordance with the usual rule, your previous service will not count for superannuation purposes". In other words, while *reversing* Lord Curzon's dismissal of Young, MacDonald and the Foreign Office officials, normally subordinate to him, were *continuing* the penalty inflicted by Curzon as part of that dismissal! The very situation which Langdon-Davies had so cogently put to Ponsonby in March had arisen in July: MacDonald had preferred to take the path of "continuity" with the Tories.

Almost needless to say, this was not the only case in which MacDonald in 1924 made such a choice: and there can be little doubt that it was precisely because Young's defiance of tradition had taken place over relations with Soviet Russia that Prime Minister and Foreign Secretary MacDonald joined in this continued and sordid piece of petty victimisation.

However, Young could hardly continue the struggle in his position. As he wrote to an old Foreign Office friend in January, 1943: "When my few savings grew shorter and shorter, and I was saddled with the responsibility for tomorrow's breakfast for a Russian wife, father-in-law and maid who had lost both their country and their all, I had to swallow my principles, and Ponsonby got me back".

So on July 7,1924, he replied to the Foreign Office that he accepted the offer made to him, on the terms stated therein, "with due appreciation". There followed another two months' delay, the necessary formalities having being completed by August 28, before—after Young had had to remind the Foreign Office on September 24—he was at last informed on October 4 that, while it was proposed "eventually" to assign him for service in Russia, it was not yet practicable to appoint British Consular officers there, and therefore he had been selected for service as Vice-Consul at Sofia.

Young left London for Bulgaria on October 24. This was only five days before the General Election, at which Labour was defeated and a Conservative Government returned to office. Thus even the grudging form of his reinstatement, with eleven years of his service from 1907 to 1918 counting for nothing, was accepted by him just in time—since it could hardly be doubted that the incoming Foreign Secretary would have reverted to Curzon's policy in this respect, as he did in much more fateful ways.

PART VI

15

When Young was appointed to Sofia, Bulgaria was still in the grip of the White Terror which began with the Fascist coup d'état engineered by Tsar Boris and his landowner and financier supporters the previous year. The repressions had been intensified after the suppression of the workers' and peasants' rising, led by the Communist Party, in September, 1923. Moreover the armed forces on which the Bulgarian Government relied had as their most reactionary core large numbers of White officers, remnants of the Denikin and Wrangel forces, who had fled from Soviet Russia after their defeat by the Red Army.

Thus Young was plunged into an atmosphere not entirely unlike that with which he would have been surrounded at Novorossiisk in 1919.

However in 1924-25, especially after the Conservative victory in the recent British elections, this was an atmosphere general throughout Eastern Europe, and Young had no choice but to make the best of it. In June, 1925, he was once again given "local rank" as full Consul. Probably it was a relief for him to take up the ordinary duties of his office: of course they were far more restricted than they had been at Archangel, since in Sofia there was a British Legation with an accredited Minister. Young became active as honorary President of the local residents' English-Speaking Club at Sofia, and devoted considerable time to arranging its library. The routine inspection of the Consulate by a Foreign Ofice inspector-general produced a favourable report a year after his appointment, and he received a letter of appreciation for his work from Sir Austen Chamberlain, now Foreign Secretary (December 24, 1925).

But his second year at Sofia was clouded by domestic trouble. His wife Varvara had been deeply shocked by the long period of Young's unemployment after the promising start to his career, as well as by his championship of better relations with the Soviet Government, whom she regarded with abhorrence as responsible for the loss of her family property. Very soon after their arrival she began to frequent the society of the Russian White emigrants in Sofia, and so far as possible avoided receiving the British colony at the Consulate. In June, 1925, she left for a visit to an aunt in Belgrade, and Young never saw her again. In 1926 she went to Paris with a Russian ex-officer, whom she married as soon as Young divorced her in 1929. It was characteristic of Young that he had a small house built at Varna for her father, with whom he was on very friendly terms, and made him an allowance until his death in 1937. He himself bought a villa there, hoping it might be available for his retirement in due course.

Some time after his divorce Young married again. The lady, Nina Sergeyevna Grinevich, was the daughter of the Marshal of Nobility in the Poltava province, a substantial landowner with estates totalling 12,000 acres at Konstantinograd (Poltava uyezd), and a member of the Duma. Nina Sergeyevna had been married at 17 to an officer in the Denikin army, who had died of typhus at Kherson during the White retreat in 1920. She reached Bulgaria the same year. There she was joined, first by her father who found employment as nightwatchman at a mill, and later, in 1923, by her mother, in whose care Nina Sergeyevna's two-year old son had been left in Russia to avoid the perils of the retreat. She herself worked in Sofia at the Inter-Allied Control Commission and then at the United States Consulate. It was at a reception for the foreign colony that Young first met her in December 1925, and began visiting the family in their crowded attic, to play records of classical music to her parents—"and with always something to eat", as Mrs Young recalled years later, in telling of their great poverty in those days. They were married in the Russian Church at Sofia in October, 1929.

Obviously Young's experiences at the hands of the British establishment, and the support he had had from the Labour Party, had not shaken his strictly "non-political" principles, including his acceptance of the old Russian aristocracy.

Their honeymoon was spent in a round tour of the Mediterranean, beginning at Venice and ending at the Black Sea coast. At Varna they were met by the Vice-Consul with a cable informing Young that he was appointed Consul at Malaga, in Spain. He served there from the end of 1929 until the spring of 1933.

Malaga, with its beautiful climate and easy conditions, seemed a sudden paradise for Mrs Young in particular, after her years of poverty, anxiety and hard physical work. Young himself had two especially memorable experiences. On April 1, 1931, the British aircraft carrier *Glorious* collided with a French banana steamer *Florida* while its 27 planes with their 42 personnel were in the air. One of the British sailors was killed, while the pilots received instructions to land at Malaga: on the *Florida* there was "considerable loss of life" (*Times* Law Reports, July 13-16, 1931). The Ambassador in Madrid was unable to find any officials at the Ministries concerned, and so was Young at Malaga (it was Holy week). Young therefore had to get permits himself from the airport office, while his wife had to rush to the shops to buy the pilots essential clothes: they had been flying only in shorts and singlets. Young as Consul took the burial service in the English Church—the only one in Spain. It was an extremely difficult situation, and the Ambassador wrote to him: "It is greatly to your credit that you were able to deal with it almost single-handed". Tributes to his "tact and expedition" were expressed by Foreign Secretary Arthur Henderson (April 24, 1931) and thanks for making "the many arrangements which became necessary" by the Admiralty (July 28).

The other experience was at the time of the overthrow of the Spanish monarchy and the establishment of the Republic. Malaga was one of the strongholds of Republicanism, and Young evidently gave a valuable analysis of the events there, for which again he received Henderson's special thanks (June 29, 1932). A dispute with the secretary of the British Club in 1932, which came to the ears of the Foreign Office, again produced an unexpected unoffical tribute, this time from the Consular Department of the Foreign Office, the chief of which in a private letter described Young, approving his attitude, as "an excellent official".

From Malaga he was transferred to Basel (Switzerland), where after some leave he served from April, 1934, until December, 1939.

This post was once more, in its own way, as much a key point for British policy as Archangel had been, in very different circumstances. First and foremost, it was practically on the border between Switzerland and Germany, where Hitler had come to power in 1933. This gave the city extreme political importance, if only because of the problems of legal and illegal communications with Germany. Secondly, it was the seat of one of the most important financial institutions between the two world wars—the Bank for International Settlements, established in 1930 by the British, French, Italian, Belgian, Japanese and German central banks, together with a group of the most powerful American banks, headed by Morgans. And thirdly, these two facts imposed once more duties on the Consulate which normally would have fallen to the British Legation — but could not do so, because the Legation was at Berne.

As regards the first aspect, Young had to deal with refugees from Nazi rule—particularly Jews—coming over the frontier by various clandestine means. So far as Britain was concerned, the Government had laid down a quota of visas to be granted: but Young's sensitive nature would not brook such restrictions, and he issued many more visas than the number authorised. A report by the Foreign Office Inspector-General of Consulates of July 29, 1939, referred to Young's issuing of some half a dozen visas for Rhodesia to German refugees. This had been done "in good faith", but his delay in answering the British Minister's request for a report (January 13, 1939) "showed a lack of judgment" (an unintentional echo of the comments made on Young's stand twenty years before, but very natural at the time when the British Government was pursuing its policy of appeasement of the Nazis).

What lay behind this "lack of judgement", however, can be seen from a passage in one of the very few letters of his at the time which have survived. One of those responsible for the the reception of the Jewish refugees at the time wrote to Young's widow, many years later:[138] "Many owe their lives to him, though they did not know him and never saw him...He did it all so modestly, quietly and wisely that for fully four years (1934-1937) I was convinced that he did not know or suspect what was going on in his Consulate at Basel—yet I used to go there day after day. Only in 1962—25 years later—did he say, in reply to my letter: "I knew exactly about your cooperation with my staff at St. Jacobstrasse: I knew everything and kept quiet. As a pacifist and anti-Nazi, I was delighted that we could help these innocent condemned people'."

The meetings of the Bank for International Settlements, which dealt particularly with the application of the reparations policy of the Allies, brought special duties of "representation" to the Consulate. Among the guests at Young's official parties during these years were Montagu Norman (Bank of England), Schacht (Deutsche Bank) and their colleagues, as well as leading figures in the Swiss banking world. In addition, representatives of the big chemical trusts—La Roche, Geiger, I.C.I. also often met at Basel, and from time to time had to be entertained at the Young's house. In these circumstances, naturally, the whole Consular Corps at Basel and the substantial British colony also required entertainment. To Mrs. Young devolved most of the duties of organisation in this sphere—which meant that, unlike his experiences elsewhere, Young was "unable to save a penny at Basel", she wrote. Once more Young became president of the local residents' English-Speaking Club, although he was unable to spare much time for its activity.

Ordinary Consular duties of course had to be carried on. In this connection a letter from Lord Halifax of November 8, 1938, presents some interest. The Foreign Office conveyed to Young "a warm expression of his thanks for the cumulative index of Foreign Office circulars to His Majesty's Consular Service" which Young had compiled: it would be of great value in revising the standard instructions to Consuls. The Inspector-General mentioned earlier commented on the improved appearance of the Consulate—"for Mr

138. Dr. M. Newiasky to Mrs. Nina Young, May 24, 1967.

Consul Young insists on a clean and tidy office...He has devoted much time and method to improving the appearance and the routine of his staff". Young was "in contact with the bankers and the leaders of industry" said the Inspector. Mrs Young was "of more cheerful temperament than her husband, and she is evidently popular socially".

But the conclusion he drew was that Young "is no longer the man for this frontier post". One could understand this opinion. As long ago as 1936 (his wife wrote) Young had decided that another war was coming, and had dropped the practice of making occasional trips across the frontier into Germany. He also was certain that Bulgaria under her then rulers would join Hitler in war, and therefore that he would not be able to retire, when the time came, to the little villa at Varna as he had hoped. Having six months' leave due to him that year, he used it to visit South Africa, where he had friends, in order to find some suitable place to which to retire before the war came. At the same time he gave his wife £100 to travel round Europe visiting her many relatives — all Russian emigrants, of course — since there might be no more chance of doing so if war overtook the world, or if the Youngs retired to South Africa. Moreover, as time went on he became more and more pessimistic in this respect. The Inspector wrote: "I found Mr Consul Young in a state of extreme nervous depression, suffering from sleeplessness and melancholia. The local doctor diagnosed his complaint as 'dépression circulaire': and as Mr Young seemed to have temporarily lost his nerve and his power of decision, my first concern was to persuade him to take a holiday. He left for the South of France early this month, on four weeks' leave". Then followed the remark already quoted about "this frontier post".

Indirectly, another ray of light pointing to the cause of his depression is contained in a letter Young wrote to the Foreign Office on September 14, 1939. The Foreign Office had told him that there was a possibility of a post for him as Consul-General at Luanda (Portuguese West Africa, as it was then, i.e Angola). Young wrote that he was ready to go there, but would like to be allowed first to use up the balance of his leave. "With the end of appeasement I feel reborn, and confident not only to hold the fort until help comes, but also—with adequate staff—to carry on this job to success at least no worse than any newcomer". Then followed a passage which, in the prevailing mood of hostility to the USSR among official circles in London in the autumn of 1939, could well seem to them a dangerous reversion to the "kink" attributed to him twenty years before. "Now that the Russian hens of 1918-1919 have finally come home to roost, why not let bygones be bygones and combine efficiency with generosity?"[139]

139. F.O. 371, vol. 3338.

Once again in this respect Young was very much in advance of his time; and the cold comment on his letter was: "We cannot consider Mr Young's feelings". Accordingly, he received in October the formal offer of his appointment to Luanda, "on the way to South Africa where you want to retire". In December, 1939, the Youngs left Basel for England, and reached Luanda in May, 1940. There they had a comfortable official residence, but Young had at first no Vice-Consul. Consequently for several months his wife had to help him "with floods of cypher telegrams, often until 2 a.m.".

On December 27, 1940, his retirement fell due, and he left Luanda for Cape Town. Five months later he and his wife settled at Somerset West—a smiling, very English-looking little community, with a largely English population, some five miles from the sea, in a green countryside between the foothills of two mountain ranges.

The pension awarded to Young in May, 1941, by the Treasury was the far from princely sum of £235 a year, with an additional bonus of £699. He had been in the Consular Service since 1908, a total of 34 years less the five years of unemployment. But even of the 29 years of active employment only 17—from 1924 onwards—were counted for pension. He had from beginning to end of his working life no private income, and only when his father died did he receive a legacy of £8,000. Of course his property at Varna was lost when the second world war began. Young had written to the Foreign Office on December 31, 1940, asking whether the question of his pension rights might not now be reconsidered. The frigid reply was that he had accepted reinstatement in 1924 on the understanding that his previous service (1907-1919) should not count for superannuation purposes, and "it is regretted that it is not now possible to reopen the matter".[140]

Of necessity Mrs Young had to seek employment herself, and almost at once found it in the wartime Censorship Department at Cape Town, where she worked until the end of the war, fully four years.

Young noticed at once the contrast between the lives and working conditions of the Africans and the life of the white man, whether running the country or living in the town. He wrote in 1943 to the friend already mentioned: "If this, plus Hong Kong, Malaya, Singapore, not to mention Jamaica, Kenya, etc. (pre-war scandals now conveniently forgotten) really represents the British Empire and our Sacred Trust to the Native Races, etc. etc., then the sooner the British Empire is liquidated, the better". This was a close echo of what another Englishman, Wilfrid Scawen Blunt, long ago also a diplomat, whose eyes had been opened to the realities of the "White

140. Foreign Office letter K4185/1509/236 of May 2, 1941.

Man's Burden", was writing at the same time.[141] But of course at sixty, without Blunt's means and with his own special handicaps, Young was unable physically to undertake Blunt's crusade.

Instead, he cultivated his garden. "Instead of a 'semi-detached' in a second-rate seaside resort, I have nearly an acre, and a capacious and comfortable house in the middle there of which, even without the sunshine, Bougainvillea, fruit-trees, etc. might well be the envy of many an inhabitant of the 'best' part of Chislehurst, and in one corner of which a baker's dozen of obliging hens provide an average of 7 eggs a day, all the year round, at a price ranging from 1/6 to 4/6 (quite recently) a dozen...So here I am, toiling more or less happily from sunrise to sunset to make at any rate my little bit of God's world better than I found it", he wrote. In this way he was able to add a little to his meagre pension. He turned his hand also to restoring furniture, cleaning pictures, and small investments in antiques, cycling for miles to outlying farms for the purpose. At Basel he had begun collecting coins, and he continued at Somerset West, helping to found a Numismatic Society there: his drawing-room was well-known for its massive range of coin cabinets. He dressed roughly, in an environment which judged of people by Victorian standards—"but everybody knows I am a gentleman", he commented in no less Victorian language. His friends recall that he always had his pockets full of sweets for the African children. In *Who's Who* he described his recreation as "thinking and reading, antiques, landscape gardening". And at 84, as mentioned earlier, he was still reading Latin poetry for pleasure.

For his thinking, the passage about the British Empire quoted above was typical of one aspect. Another may be illustrated from the same letter: "It is a pity that there should be this 'unfortunate suspicion' between England and her *now* gallant Ally—tho' there doesn't seem to be much on the part of the British 'common' people". His deep feeling that irreparable injury had been done, and was still being done, to British interests by the inveterate hostility of the ruling classes to Russia ever since 1917, was unshaken. It moved him more than once after the war to write letters to the South African newspapers when the Soviet Union was being vilified. Whenever more or less reliable books about the USSR and its history came his way, he discussed them earnestly with his closest friends.

One of them, a schoolmaster, wrote of Young:[142]

> "I first noticed his tall spare figure in the early 50's. His white goatee beard and direct bearing would have made him stand out

141. I venture to refer the reader to the lecture on Blunt in my "British Foreign Policy and its Critics" (London, 1969).

142. Leslie Webb to Andrew Rothstein, April 12, 1971.

everywhere. Nodding acquaintance ripened into friendship, and bit by bit I learned something of his extraordinary history.

"A mutual interest in politics and diplomatic history encouraged him to speak of his past. A good many years passed before he developed sufficient confidence to entrust to me his own manuscript of the great events in which he had been involved.

"This was in 1954. And it was with a strange exhilaration that I began to read the manuscript early one evening. Douglas Young had told me that no eyes other than his own had read these papers from the time of his reinstatement by the Foreign Office in 1924. I finished reading in the early hours, conscious of the historical importance of the documents in my hand.

"I asked the writer why, now that the heat and passion of the deplorable decision to intervene in North Russia had largely subsided, he did not publish the material. He replied that he still felt bound by his undertaking to the Foreign Office on reinstatement not to communicate to the Press in any way about the events in which he was involved.

"In this his attitude was one that I would have expected from the Edwardian gentleman he was. His ideas and standards of behaviour were firmly based on the prevailing codes of the pre-1914 world. He had a great reverence for scholarship, high standards of moral rectitude, a sense of honour which made the keeping of one's word a matter of importance. Two world wars had left him with a horror of the mindless violence of the twentieth century. Yet he was no out-and-out pacifist: he loved England far too much for complete rejection of the right of self-defence.

"Washed up on this far African shore, he remained the English gentleman—and by reason of his marriage, a Russian gentleman too, speaking and writing fluent Russian. There was a suggestion of Chekhov in his appearance and character. Although he was liberal in his sympathies, it would be untrue to represent him as a complete egalitarian. He was in many ways an 'elitist', who believed in the aristocracy of intelligence and learning. However, he was an 'elitist' to whom responsibility and duty came before privilege. It was this feeling that estranged him from the traditional ruling class of Britain, and placed him in that widest of movements, the Radical tradition.

"In the last years of his life illness often depressed him, and on the occasions when I was able to see him he returned again and again to the subject of his papers. Would anyone want to publish them?"

In 1965, at 83, Young suffered a first heart attack, and from that time was confined to an upper room. Nevertheless from time to time he ventured downstairs. On April 5, 1967, however there was a sudden clot on the brain, and he lost consciousness. His mind wandered for over three weeks. Finally, on April 30, he briefly returned to consciousness and took Communion from the Anglican Rector of Somerset West. He died the same evening. His ashes were deposited in the columbarium of the Anglican Church.

He had spent his last weeks arranging his papers, which were found in perfect order.

"I was certainly never a yes-man, not since 1918 at any rate", he wrote in 1943 to the friend mentioned earlier: and those qualifying words about the turning-point in his life mark the outstanding characteristic which made Douglas Young one of the most remarkable people of his time. Up to 1918 he had been bred in uprightness and honourable behaviour, trained for conscientious and indeed devoted service to his country, as he understood it in the light of British Civil Service traditions. Then, so rapidly that he had great difficulty in following what was happening, he discovered in the course of 1918 that, in the name of patriotic service, he was required to practise dishonourable dealing as though it were honourable, and follow crooked ways in place of uprightness. The very unswerving honesty with which he followed the dictates of conscience made him revolt against what he was expected to do. There were few other foreigners in Russia at the time to raise the voice of protest. There were some intrepid journalists—the Americans John Reed, Albert Rhys Williams, Louise Bryant and Bessie Beatty: Arthur Ransome and Morgan Philips Price in Britain: René Marchand in France — but none of them faced more than a short period of unpopularity for their exposures. There were also a handful of courageous men who held semi-official positions in Russia for their respective countries— Captain Jacques Sadoul and Lieut. Pierre Pascal, members of the French Military Mission: Colonel Raymond Robins, chief of the American Red Cross Mission: later on William C. Bullitt, sent to Russia on a mission of enquiry by Secretary of State Lansing with the approval of Premier Lloyd George. But Sadoul as a Socialist was able for several years to find asylum in Russia from persecution in his own country, until the worst was over: Robins was a prosperous businessman who could return to his normal pursuits with only a minimum of inconvenience: Bullitt could take refuge from his disgust at official tergiversation in a life of wealthy and cultured leisure, until his own convictions had changed acceptably for the American establishment.

But Young was earlier than all of these in his determined protest: he stood to lose more than any of them — and he did. Like Sir Robert

Bruce Lockhart, in those same years, he knew that he "was living in a movement which was likely to assume even greater proportions in history than the French revolution". Like Lockhart, he knew that his views "were unpalatable to the British Government". But Lockhart, as he wrote himself, "lacked the moral courage to resign and to take a stand which would have exposed me to the odium of the vast majority of my countrymen". [143] Young was well aware of the risk that he was running. He told Francis Meynell, then editor of the *Herald*, that he would probably be dismissed for the article of December 14, 1918. But he took the risk. The Foreign Office comments on his papers show that, if he was not exposed by his superiors to public "odium", it was only because they knew that the majority of their countrymen would be more outraged by the truth about the intervention campaign than by Young's breach of discipline and fearless break with tradition.[144]

---

143. *Memoirs of a British Agent* (Penguin, London, 1950) pp. 284-285.

144. This, incidentally, was well illustrated several months later when Lieut.-Col. John Sherwood Kelly, V.C. was put on trial by court-martial on October 28, 1919, for writing to the press and to the Trades Union Congress denouncing the Archangel "relief expedition," which in reality was sent to start a new offensive against the Red Army.

INDEX